RACE AND THE POLITICS OF DECEPTI

Race and the Politics of Deception

The Making of an American City

Christopher Mele

NEW YORK UNIVERSITY PRESS

New York

NEW YORK UNIVERSITY PRESS
New York
www.nyupress.org

References to Internet websites (URLs) were accurate at the time of writing. Neither the author nor New York University Press is responsible for URLs that may have expired or changed since the manuscript was prepared.

ISBN: 978-1-4798-6609-0 (hardback)
ISBN: 978-1-4798-8043-0 (paperback)

For Library of Congress Cataloging-in-Publication data, please contact the
Library of Congress.

New York University Press books are printed on acid-free paper, and their binding materials are chosen for strength and durability. We strive to use environmentally responsible suppliers and materials to the greatest extent possible in publishing our books.

Manufactured in the United States of America

10 9 8 7 6 5 4 3 2 1

Also available as an ebook

To my mother, Amy

CONTENTS

ACKNOWLEDGMENTS

My home institution, the University at Buffalo (UB), provided a supportive environment for the research and writing of this book. Grants awarded by UB's Civic Engagement Fellowship and Baldy Center for Law and Social Policy provided funding for interviews and archival research. The Baldy Center funded a manuscript workshop at the American Sociological Association annual meeting in Chicago in 2015. I am greatly indebted to Professors Rodney Coates, Cedric Johnson, and Michael Maly who signed on to the manuscript workshop, read a complete first draft, and provided me with critical comments and supportive encouragement over three amazing hours. My understanding of the sociology of race improved immensely thanks to Nancy Denton, David Wilson, and several other excellent scholars who attended a workshop on new forms of racial segregation that fellow UB sociologist Robert Adelman and I co-organized at the Baldy Center. The workshop provided an opportunity for all of us to try out new ideas and led to the publication of a co-edited book, *Race, Space, and Exclusion: Segregation and Beyond in Metropolitan America* (2015).

I am indebted to several individuals who have provided many different kinds of support in seeing this project through from start to finish. Margaret Johnson, the coordinator of the Delaware County Historical Society Research Library is exceptionally knowledgeable of all things Chester. The research librarians at UB, the University of Delaware, Widener University, Temple University, and Swarthmore College were always accommodating and helpful. Over the course of research and writing this book, I benefited from the support of Errol Meidinger and Laura Wirth of the Baldy Center and steady encouragement from my colleagues and graduate students in the Departments of Sociology and

Geography at UB, particularly Robert Adelman, Aaron Lee, and Peng Gao. Many thanks as well to Kelly Crean and Diane Holfelner for putting up with my many requests. I am especially grateful to Jean Kaplan for all her hard work and diligence as an amazingly skillful editor. I am very thankful for the support and encouragement of Ilene Kalish, executive editor, and Caelyn Cobb, assistant editor at NYU Press.

My friends and family members graciously tolerated my many years of obsession with anything to do with Chester. I am particularly grateful for the love, support, and kindness of Charles Hallmark, Genevieve Hinkle, Kelly Hinkle, Emilie Broderick, Mary Miller, Monica Alvarez, Amy Taylor, Val Marie Johnson, Diane Levy, and Victor Mirando. I thank you all.

PREFACE

My memories of Chester, Pennsylvania, stretch back to my early childhood despite the fact that I did not visit the city until I was in my late forties. I grew up in the suburbs of North Wilmington, Delaware, a mere fourteen miles and barely twenty minutes south of Chester on Interstate 95. But my life was worlds apart from that of people in Chester, as was the case in most of the 1970s suburbs of single-family homes, wooded parks, and shopping malls of cities like Philadelphia, Camden, and Wilmington. Or so I was told. When I was a child, acting up or misbehaving often came with an admonition from adults that I would "be sent to Chester." A high school classmate whose uncle was a Chester police officer told stories of found bodies, drug world shoot-outs, gang wars, and most memorably, entire neighborhoods where even the police dared not go. When I was sixteen, a massive fire consumed Chester's Wade toxic chemical dump for days. I can recall watching live news coverage of towering flames seeming to engulf the Commodore Barry Bridge and highway officials' fears that the steel structure might buckle under the intense heat. Twenty years later and having moved away, I read in a follow-up news article that nearly a quarter of the two hundred firefighters had suffered from deadly cancers due to their exposure to chemicals leaking at the dump.

My first visit to Chester peaked my curiosity as a sociologist, which eventually led to the research for this book. Caring for my aging mother included the first of many trips to the Harrah's Chester casino and racetrack, which opened in 2007 and quickly attracted senior citizens drawn to its rows of blaring slot machines and the elusive promise of jackpots. It was the first time my mother had been to Chester since the 1940s. Back then the city was the Delaware Valley nightlife destination, where a multitude of dance clubs, music halls, and corner bars served up alcohol and entertainment well into the early morning hours. Her nostalgia mimicked that of thousands of white suburbanites, including those who visit the website OldChesterPA.com to view and post photographs of the "good old days." To me, the city seemed a jumbled mix of land uses, each a testimony to a different period of urban change in the past one hundred years. The new Harrah's, resembling a warehouse bathed in pink neon, sat across a narrow street from a minimum security state prison (constructed of pink bricks). The remainder of the waterfront housed metal shops, a recycling facility, and an energy-from-waste plant that incinerated trash generated by all of Delaware County and some municipalities in the tri-state region (including since 2015 New York City). Near the Commodore Barry Bridge, where the Wade fire had blazed out of control for days, the massive, Beaux Arts-style Chester Waterside Station of the Philadelphia Electric Company had been repurposed as an office building and anchor for Rivertown, a planned upscale mixed-use district. Across the Industrial Highway, sits the city proper, with its partially abandoned downtown commercial district, barren and overgrown lots, and neighborhoods of tidy redbrick row houses. In many ways, Chester's past and present differ little from any number of small- to medium-sized former industrial cities in the northeastern United States, among them Camden, Wilmington, Baltimore, and Newark.

On our return home, we spotted a Chester Yes! billboard along the Industrial Highway proclaiming a new, revitalized Chester anchored along the waterfront was in the making. Not the Chester of my childhood mind's eye, populated with images of violence, fire, and drug wars, but not that of my mother either, of busy shopping streets, brightly lit diners, and crowded saloons. That the deindustrialized, minority city is imagined quite vividly (but incompletely and more likely, erroneously) from a white, suburban perspective is of little surprise and of little research interest to me. Nor have I been interested in unearthing the "real Chester" in some effort to correct the middle-class, suburban myth of the minority ghetto—a project that might well lead to another incomplete, albeit more sympathetic, reification (as I discuss in chapter 6). Instead, what piqued my interest was how the range of negative images and associations—Chester's notoriety, the stereotypical view of the majority of individuals and families who live there—might play into a complex and surreal politics of urban development that could produce a prison, a casino, one of the country's largest waste incinerators, a soccer stadium, and the promise of upscale housing and shopping. As I spent more time learning about the city and its past, I discovered how the politics of Chester's development pivoted around race and, specifically, ideas about race and racial minorities. It soon became clear to me that the forces that transformed Chester's neighborhoods, downtown, the waterfront, and its surrounding suburbs were articulated, justified, and enabled by an urban politics that relied on the manipulation of race—or more precisely, fictions and falsehoods that comprise the images, rhetoric, and ideologies of race. It also became evident that the manipulation of race was a consistent, intentional, and deliberate strategy in the local politics of development. In short, how might the employment of race as a convoluted yet useful set of ideas about "others" function as a strategy in the development of Chester? This book is an attempt to answer that by digging into the city's past and exploring episodes in which the representations of minorities were intentionally manipulated to foster spatial changes in the city and the region, moments in which the saliency of race had little if anything to do with the ordinary experiences of people who lived in Chester and everything to do with the exaggeration and just plain falsification of impressions and representations of race. Although this book focuses on one city, there is little to suggest that the enduring significance of race to urban politics is unique to Chester.

The stories presented in this book come from a mix of data sources and research methods. In addition to spending lengths of time in Chester interviewing officials, residents (current and former), and community leaders, my research benefited from a wealth of resources produced by local historians, librarians, scholars, and journalists. My understanding of Chester's past is in large part indebted to my reading of the historian

John J. McLarnon III's dissertation and masterful book *Ruling Subur-bia: John J. McClure and the Republican Machine in Delaware County, Pennsylvania* (2003). Richard Harris's *Politics and Prejudice: Small-Town Blacks Battle a Corrupt System* (2008) documents the struggles of Chester's black community against the excesses of white politics outlined by McLarnon. As a hotbed of civil rights activism, the coverage of Chester loomed large throughout the Papers of the National Association for the Advancement of Colored People (NAACP), made available to me at the University at Buffalo (UB) library. My work benefited from multiple visits to the Delaware County Historical Society library which houses a vast archive of photographs, newspaper clippings, personal accounts, and secondary resources about Chester and Delaware County. Another archive, the George Raymond Papers at Widener University's Wolfgram Memorial Library, were similarly valuable to retelling key parts of the city's past. I also learned much about Chester's past and present from formal meetings and ad hoc conversations with residents, leaders of civic associations, and local church officials.

Race Strategies and the Politics of Urban Development

Each day tens of thousands of people pass through the city of Chester, Pennsylvania, making their way to destinations along the mid-Atlantic seaboard from Boston, Massachusetts, to Washington, D.C. Interstate 95 and Amtrak's Northeast Regional passenger rail line cut right through Chester, and most travelers, speeding along in cars or in trains, are oblivious to yet another blurry patch of redbrick row houses and old, abandoned factories seen repeatedly along their routes. The same holds true for most commuters, shoppers, and others who live in Greater Philadelphia and have very few reasons to think about (much less stop in) Chester. For many of them, Chester is the city "that used to be nice," a forgotten, dangerous, and mostly deserted place to be avoided, or a highway marker just south of Philadelphia, north of the Delaware state line, and on the edge of leafy and very wealthy Delaware County.

Since 2005 local economic development officials, politicians, business leaders, and developers have worked tirelessly to make Chester less a place to drive through, ignore, or intentionally avoid and more of a destination for middle-class visitors and eventually residents. Their strategy has been to capitalize on the city's location along major transportation arteries and open a riverfront casino, a waterfront esplanade park, and a soccer stadium for a major league expansion team financed by a mix of public dollars, tax abatements, and private investment. Suburban Delaware Valley gamblers now flock to the casino in great numbers, quickly moving from the Interstate highway to a covered parking garage. Soccer fans see Chester as home to their team, the Philadelphia Union, and celebrate the new stadium as proof of the growing popularity of the sport in the United States. Chester's revival appears on track—as long as all

Map of Chester and the Eastern Seaboard of the United States.

eyes remain focused on the new developments along the waterfront and are not diverted by the crumbling neighborhoods nearby.

The casino and the stadium sit in striking visual and social contrast to the rest of Chester, the small city left behind long ago—the city people travel through at high speeds, the city people ignore, or, as they have for decades, consciously avoid. Among the residential streets and in the downtown core, the consequences of decades of political neglect and economic decline are readily apparent. The city's landscape is peppered with dilapidated but still occupied row houses, countless empty storefronts, and abandoned lots, with an occasional corner grocery and a small number of bars, taverns, and liquor stores. Of the thirty-six thousand people who live in Chester, 80 percent of whom are black, more than a third are "officially" poor, and a quarter over the age of twenty-five have earned less than a high school diploma. Chester consistently ranks high in official federal and state statistics for street gang activity, assaults

Map of the Chester waterfront.

and homicides, poorly performing schools, long-term unemployment, and sagging community health levels. In February 2015 Neighborhood Scout, an Internet website that provides crime, school, and real estate data for cities and neighborhoods across the United States, ranked Chester the second most dangerous city in the country.[1] Chester is Pennsylvania's poorest city and is located in the state's wealthiest county.

For most of Chester's poor, black residents, the leisure enclave rising along the waterfront is the source of many changes but few benefits to their daily lives. The casino and the stadium employ residents but primarily in low-wage service sector jobs—as janitors, security guards, and restaurant staff. For most, the waterfront is an off-limits enclave meant for suburbanites to gamble, see a soccer game, or attend a corporate-sponsored event. A casino and a Major League Soccer stadium can hardly be considered meaningful urban revitalization for a disadvantaged city with crumbling infrastructure and no supermarket, "big box" store, or thriving small business district. As a twenty-seven-year-old resident told a *New York Times* reporter covering the city's revival, "We've got a casino, a prison and now a stadium but we don't have a recreation center or even a McDonald's in this city."[2] If anything, the waterfront has further confined its residents to the inner city, as past uses of the waterfront—from hanging out and meeting up to barbequing and fishing—are now unwelcome or simply prohibited. Today, high-tech surveillance and new crime control initiatives police the public spaces along the waterfront and increasingly, the city proper. For young people, particularly young black males, ordinary behaviors such as hanging out or congregating on a street corner, have become coded as suspicious and potentially threatening to the success of the city's regeneration. In the politics of urban development, the residents of Chester themselves seem to stand in the way of the city's reinvention as a destination for middle-class suburbanites.

Even though Chester's black community feels left behind, further marginalized, and increasingly scrutinized, city officials and developers are quick to contend otherwise. They argue that the new Chester promises residential, work, and entertainment spaces open and accessible to all—

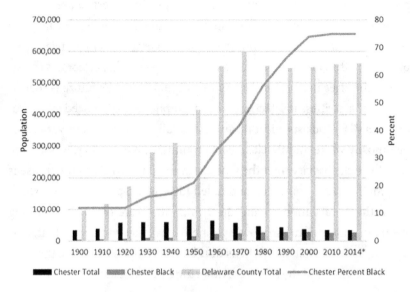

Populations of Chester and Delaware County, 1900–2014.

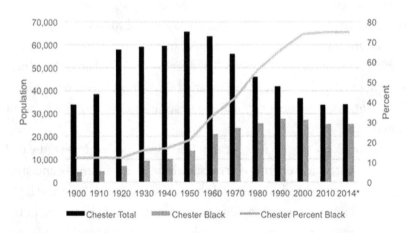

Black population of Chester, 1900–2014.

provided they can afford to participate. They claim waterfront redevelopment benefits the entire city despite the fact that it provides few tangible resources to tackle long-standing social problems or to meet needs prioritized by the community. Infused with a language that celebrates the allure of the "free market" and economic capital, the city's future is shaped by leisure activities, spectacles, and consumption, as evidenced by its "rediscovery" by tourists, visitors, and eventually residents from varied, albeit mostly white middle-class, backgrounds. The new Chester is a more socially inclusive city than the Chester of the past. To claim otherwise is to remain stuck in outdated and failed ideas of urban renewal in which institutional racism, bias, and discrimination were recognized among the main causes of urban poverty. Chester has moved beyond that, embracing a post-racial, nonpolitics of urban development, where the winner is "the city" and the losers are unfortunate individuals—but not entire communities.

This image of Chester as a city embracing all things entrepreneurial and welcoming diversity helps legitimize the current progrowth model of urban development politics in which most of the city's residents are left out in the cold. Race—or more precisely in this case the denial of the salience of race and racism—serves as a useful strategy to normalize a city's ambitions for economic development at the expense of meaningful community development. The ideology of racial color blindness sorts out and makes sense of the apparent disconnect between the everyday realities of the inner city and the upscale ambitions of the adjacent waterfront.

This book focuses on how local political leaders, developers, the real estate industry, and other powerful stakeholders intentionally and strategically employ the ideologies and rhetoric of race to facilitate and legitimize certain types of urban development and to exclude others. In the current progrowth politics of urban development, the ideology of color blindness comprises a *race strategy* that facilitates exclusionary urban redevelopment and, in turn, marks a clear distinction between economic and community development.[3] Chester's redevelopment is meant to attract middle-class, suburban consumers. Redevelopment is not meant to address the collective needs of poor black residents of a city reeling from decades of racial segregation and deindustrialization. This exclusion of community needs is enabled by the ideology of color blindness, which is politically useful because it rejects the contemporary relevance of systematic racism and explains urban inequality as the product of "nonracial dynamics."[4] The social problems of urban poverty, inferior housing, chronic unemployment, and deficient education are largely attributable to individuals or their collective, cultural deficiencies but not to institutional or systemic racism. The race strategy of color blindness provides ideological cover, however thin, for urban development policies and practices that exclude and further marginalize the minority poor without the appearance of doing so.

Color-blind racial ideology is strategic to Chester's progrowth politics. The economic and social problems of the inner city are seen as the remaining vestiges of inefficient or hindered market forces or the private and unfortunate consequences of the choices and behaviors of residents themselves. The city's poor black residents are less a community or constituency than a collection of individuals who either comply with the goals of contemporary urban development—as consumers, low-wage workers in the waterfront facilities, or simply bystanders (who neither participate nor stand in the way of revitalization)—or they are obstacles and regarded as potential security threats. The minority inner city, then, is redefined not as a place replete with systematic discrimination and exclusion but as a post-racial realm hamstrung by the deficiencies of individual self-sufficiency, responsibility for one's social welfare, and participation in the market economy. The reimagined inner city as a space devoid of problems caused by racism and racial discrimination is not epiphenomenal to contemporary urban development, it is at its core. And Chester, like many other American cities, is currently reimagined in this very way. As told in this book, Chester's past and present are consistently shaped and defined by the different uses of race as a strategy in the local politics of urban development.

Employing Race Strategies in Urban Change

The use of color blindness to shore up the stark disconnect between Chester's waterfront economic development and the minority city's community underdevelopment is but the most recent occurrence of a long-established pattern of employing race in the politics of urban development. Drawing on the history of Chester and its suburbs, this book examines how the systematic and intentional employment of race shapes urban and metropolitan spaces in older, decline belt cities of the Northeast and Midwest. Race does not merely serve as an ideological setting or context in which urban development unfolds. Instead, the rhetoric and discourses about race and racism are intentionally fused to the wide range of local political processes linked to city development—from the early formation of the urban ghetto, to suburbanization and inner city decline, to more recent attempts at revitalization. Race strategies, then, are formative in the sense that rhetoric, representations, and discourses of race are manipulated and employed by key power holders to facilitate and legitimize certain kinds of urban change over others.[5]

As the chapters in this book recount, the use of race strategies is not exceptional but forms a normalized part of doing business in the spatial development of cities and suburbs over the past century. Repeatedly, race strategies have proven to be a useful and efficient means for local political leaders and private actors to push through, accelerate, and profit from profound changes in the urban-suburban landscape. They remain effective largely because race—or more precisely, fictions about race—consistently resonate in the public consciousness, even as their meanings continue to change over time. As W. E. B. Du Bois warned in 1903, "The problem of the twentieth century is the problem of the color-line." But like most social problems, the color line in the United States has transformed in ways both intended and unforeseen, stemming from popular collective action, political economic changes, and shifts in cultural and ideological frames. Throughout the long century, issues of race—fictitious and otherwise—have continued to resonate powerfully in the media, on college campuses, in national politics, and in the local politics of space.

In the United States, the history of urban development reveals the enduring significance of race. At the city-suburb level, racial divisions are visible in most aspects of contemporary society, including policing and criminal justice, education, health care, access to financial capital, and social service provision. Progress has been made in narrowing certain dimensions of the racial divide, as evidenced by limited and uneven declines in racial segregation and in the public intolerance of blatant racial prejudice.[6] However, whether measurable racial segregation is slowly disappearing or is sustained in new, elusive ways rests on a literal, demographic interpretation of the racial divide. Such a view neglects the ideologies and rhetoric of race and racism, another dimension of the racial divide and one that can be wielded or employed strategically to shape metropolitan development. While the meanings and ideologies of race and the black-white divide have been and continue to be redefined, they nonetheless are consistently used to influence the direction, limits and possibilities of urban change.

The significance of race to the way cities are shaped and formed is not easily severed from the importance of social class inequalities. But in the politics of urban development, race is symbolically and discursively separated from class; issues of race are employed in their own right as a strategic means for local elites and governments to shape and advance the direction of metropolitan change. Class inequalities shape urban restructuring, from suburbanization to abandonment to revitalization. Yet urban restructuring is imagined, worked out, legitimated, and reconciled in an urban politics that consistently relies on the wielding and, more often than not, cynical manipulation of race and the racial divide. This book's focus on the strategic quality of race is not to deny or downplay the significance of other dimensions of race and racism to urban inequalities but rather to argue the opposite: that race so clearly, consistently, and problematically resonates in American popular culture that it is a highly useful sociocultural prism through which the politics of urban development is represented, understood, and acted on. Urban inequality and division, Georg Simmel reminds us, "is not a spatial fact with sociological consequences, but a sociological fact that forms itself spatially."[7] The utility of race in the politics of urban development will not disappear as long as the fiction of race remains a powerful (and useful) ideological basis for the way Americans perceive and react to their cities and suburbs.

The use of race in the politics of urban development has lasting chilling effects on minority communities. The utility of race strategies relies on the distortion and manipulation of race, racial groups, and purported racial behaviors. The purpose of this book is not to critique the fictive content of racial rhetoric and discourses per se but to trace their utility as a strategic means to legitimize and push through certain forms of urban change over others. Nonetheless, the stories recounted in this book document how urban politics draws from the rhetoric, ideologies, and fictions of race in an attempt to silence or speak authoritatively on behalf of "a black community" and to render invisible the actual diversity of those who reside in the city. Too often, the "noise" of urban politics drowns out the voices of various grassroots proponents of community-focused development. As the following chapters show, race strategies have often thwarted the efforts of community-based networks to shape a more progressive future for the city at different points in its history. But it would be a mistake to assume that the often-stigmatizing discourses that constitute race strategies position black residents solely as "victims" or passive agents of larger, more powerful forces. As the details in the following chapters also reveal, Chester's black residents organized and promoted their own vision of a livable city at various points and accomplished much in ways both spectacular and mundane, given the context of larger political and economic circumstances. Grassroots social movements, activist churches, local civil rights associations, block associations, and community organizations consistently fought for their constituents against the narrow agenda of powerful stakeholders in city development. The wielding (and manipulation) of race in the politics of urban development does not eliminate community populism and everyday meaningful practices on the ground in black communities. Indeed, such practices and the ordinary lives of most residents may be seen as quiet resistance to the fiction of race put forth and used by those in power.

Outline of the Book

The following five chapters examine the different uses of race strategies in the politics of urban development. The chapters are arranged chronologically from the early 1900s to the present but the book in its entirety does not present a comprehensive history of Chester. Instead, each chapter features vignettes that center around how different racial strategies are intentionally linked to changes in urban space, from racial segregation and the emergence of a black ghetto to inner city disinvestment and the more recent revitalization of the waterfront. The chapters illustrate the strategic choices available to actors at key moments, the articulation of their interests through the language of race and racism, and how opportunities to mend the racial divisions were rarely explored and often exploited.

Chapter 2, "The Racial Divide in the Making of Chester," examines how race first emerged as a strategy in the politics of city building in early twentieth-century Chester. As a consequence of the city's 1917 race riot, black and white divisions defined the spatial reorganization of the city. Segregation hardened, providing the basis for white privileges in the urban environment but not without ensuring a level of security and stability for the black community with long-lasting consequences for racial integration efforts. The chapter also tells the story of race and industrial employment and how race was used in the workplace politics of industrial unionization in the 1930s and 1940s. As the chapter shows, race emerged as a complex yet reliable political flash point in the social and spatial organization of Chester. Race became the ordering mechanism of urban change and its employment as a strategy would continue to shape the politics of city and suburban development for decades to come.

Chapter 3, "How to Make a Ghetto," examines how strategically employing racist fears became embedded and institutionalized in the postwar politics of urban and suburban segregation. During the 1950s, political leaders used the threat of integration to goad the public commitment of local whites to uphold and reproduce the city's black-white divide. In response to the growing black ghetto whites "hunkered down," taking the lead and joining forces with political and economic institutions to prevent blacks from encroaching into white neighborhoods— and eventually, suburbs. Stoking racial fears would play into the emerging interests of politicians, developers, and institutions in the promise (and profits) of the surrounding suburbs. As the chapter shows, the threat of an undoing of the racial order encouraged white flight from the city. The suburbs in turn became the convenient "spatial fix" to the pressures of racial integration. While racial prejudice and bias reflected the dominant racial ideology of white privilege at the time, chapter 3 explains how race-baiting became normalized in the politics of metropolitan expansion in the 1950s. The officially sanctioned use of racial animus and fears clearly points toward the intentionality, not the inevitability, of suburban exclusion.

Chapter 4 examines the curious circumstances surrounding Chester's part in the civil rights activism of the 1960s. Chester was a hotbed of demonstrations, protests, and boycotts to end racial segregation, earning the city the reputation of being the "Birmingham of the North."[8] But here the familiar story of 1960s black activism is anything but straightforward, as white political elites embarked on a duplicitous strategy of defending and disrupting the city's long-standing racial order. Chapter 4 picks up on the racial fears of whites that were exploited and strategically employed to the point where local political leaders were directly implicated in fomenting civil unrest. After months of demonstrations and unrest in the streets of Chester, the politics of suburban development fully exploited white anxiety over the city's collapsing racial status quo. As chapter 4 reveals, local political leaders added fuel to the smoldering racial divisions and readily profited from the consequences of

Central business district, Chester, 2015.

doing so. By 1970 the outward movement of mostly white families and small businesses and the decline in industrial employment left Chester's remaining, largely black population concentrated and isolated in an aging core with few economic options.

Chapter 5, "Five Square Miles of Hell," tells the snaking story of the city's downturn from the late 1960s to the mid-1990s. The chapter focuses on the way political and private sector elites manipulated and used the racial ideologies and rhetoric of the black underclass to drain the city's coffers and the remaining residents' meager resources. Race became the strategic means to create and reproduce a sophisticated parasitic politics of urban underdevelopment. The relatively small gains in economic and housing conditions for the city's black majority (compelled by Pennsylvania and the federal government's War on Poverty) were quickly squandered by vast municipal corruption that implicated white elites and emerging black leaders and condemned large tracts of the city to economic despair and social isolation. While the majority of the city's residents were subject to persistent crime, poverty, and unemployment, city leaders and private investors cannibalized the industrial waterfront, transforming it into one of the major toxic waste zones on the East Coast. Chapter 5 speaks to the strategic political decision to "chase smokestacks" and use race to win over the cooperation of corporations, regulatory agencies, and briefly the people of Chester.

Chapter 6, "Welcome to the 'Post-Racial' Black City," returns to contemporary development along Chester's waterfront. It sets out to explain the strategic relevance of race to making sense of and justifying the physical and symbolic disconnect between the city's minority community and the new entertainment district rising along the Delaware River. The chapter lays out the political economy of the waterfront development and demonstrates how color-blind racial ideology legitimizes the exclusion of the vast majority of the city's residents. The chapter concludes with a discussion of what may be learned from the persistent association of race and development as presented in the book. It calls for greater community stakeholder involvement that would generate the kind of urban development that is socially advantageous without furthering racial exclusion. This would require implementation of more inclusive decision-making processes. Instead of excluding the current inhabitants and further downplaying community ties to the future of urban development to attract capital and new residents, strategies should be developed that focus on revitalizing community in meaningful ways.

Racializing How Urban Spaces Are Unevenly Produced

In the 2015 inaugural edition of the journal, *Sociology of Race and Ethnicity*, the race scholar Eduardo Bonilla-Silva wrote, "Sociologists have done a pretty decent job documenting and theorizing how class . . . and gender . . . shape space and organizations. But we are behind in theorizing how race does the same."[9] The purpose of this book is to respond to this call and to interject the strategic dimensions of race into our existing understanding of the political economy of urban development. Urban sociologists and geographers have long emphasized the structural effects of racially discriminatory governmental policies on metropolitan areas and have provided detailed analyses of the effects of institutional discrimination on concentrated poverty.[10] The origin and persistence of racial segregation is clearly connected to the broader political economy of capitalism. In particular, racial discrimination has been directly tied to the workings of real estate investment and development and federal housing programs and policies.[11] But established theories of urban political economy tend to emphasize the relevance of capital flows and social class divisions at the expense of other equally important factors, including the discourses and rhetoric of race. To this end, this book should be read alongside important work on political economy to develop a broader understanding of urban development.

This book's emphasis on the politics of development, in particular the agency and intentionality behind the strategic use of race, is a necessary complement to explanations of American urban development in which structural elements of race and class are highlighted. Much of the short history of the post–World War II U.S. city is neatly condensed in a grand narrative of suburbanization, white flight, deindustrialization, and gentrification. The legacy of post–World War II discriminatory policies and actions, including governmental housing and transportation policies, institutional lending practices, and the private behaviors of realtors and home owners, is today's racial segregation and exclusion (and the subsequent costs to the health, safety, and education of minority communities). For those who emphasize the successes of the civil rights era in diminishing racial discrimination, the continued existence of inner city black ghettos is but an unfortunate by-product of revitalization efforts or simply the failure of recent urban redevelopment to deliver on its promises. There is nothing inherently wrong with these broad historical brushstrokes except that they have become convenient shorthand for otherwise complex events and processes that transpired in real time on the ground (as the chapters in this book attempt to show). Agency and intentionality are too often flattened in structural accounts of urban development. This book tries to correct that.

By focusing on a single city, this book demonstrates how race is strategically linked to the the local politics of urban development. The intentional use of vignettes (and not a complete social history) avoids a familiar case study retelling of twentieth-century urban rise and decline. That narrative, which incorporates the stories of metropolitan growth, deindustrialization, suburbanization, and gentrification and whose broad contours are indisputably correct, has been told repeatedly, so much so that a convincing inevitability can be read into the past of older American cities. Chester's story clearly ties in with the urban rise-and-decline narrative, but this book tries to avoid a standard recounting and instead reveals the sometimes unexpected and always complex interplay of context, racial categories, constraints, decisions, and choices regarding urban change in different time periods.

The ideology of race neutrality notwithstanding, racial divisions continue to shape everyday life in ordinary, spectacular, unexpected, and often tragic ways. Strategically invoking the rhetoric and ideology of race and racism is a cynical politics of manipulation, as the stories presented in this book attest. The deliberate stirring of collective anxieties, fears, and animosity through the use of racial stereotypes, racist imagery, and racially coded language is an act of power that undermines the best intentions of individuals and organizations working to solve social problems at the local level and working to create more livable cities. The use of discourses of the racial divide by political leaders and developers to further their own agendas drowns out and threatens to silence the progressive voices of grassroots political and civic institutions eager to rebuild their communities. Although the chapters that follow concentrate on the cynical use of race by those with the power and means to do otherwise, the intended objective of this book is not a pessimistic one. Pointing out the pragmatic uses of race in the politics of urban development is a troubling but necessary and modest step in the ongoing efforts to end the isolation of individuals and organizations seeking to improve their cities.

2

The Racial Divide in the Making of Chester

When World War I broke out in Europe in 1914, Chester, Pennsylvania, was "a sleepy, provincial little city through which rushed, without stopping, the more important express trains to Baltimore and Washington."[1] Three years later and as a result of a ramped up war economy, Chester was a full-fledged industrial boomtown. Between 1910 and 1920 the city's population jumped from thirty-eight thousand to fifty-eight thousand due to an influx of southern and eastern European immigrants and southern U.S. blacks. Waterfront factories making locomotives, ships, and machine parts hummed around the clock, and new stores, hotels, restaurants, and movie houses sprang up across downtown. Worker housing was woefully overcrowded and in short supply, and an antiquated infrastructure of sewers, roads, and transport groaned under the weight of increasing commerce and activity. Like most boomtowns, Chester was unprepared for the dramatic social changes that accompanied rapid growth and instigated class, ethnic, and racial divisions and tensions. And like many industrializing cities in the early twentieth century, those tensions erupted along racial lines. When a race riot broke out in the city in July 1917, Chester joined ranks with seventeen other cities that suffered racial unrest between 1915 and 1919.[2] And as in those other cities, the separation of blacks and whites in Chester's neighborhoods and workplaces hardened.

Racial segregation in northern industrial cities issued from the racial antipathy of whites toward blacks. But the hardening of segregation also reflected the fierce pragmatism of early twentieth-century machine politics bent on preserving control of the ballot box and the perks of local office. The issue of race was not of tertiary concern to political leaders and ordinary citizens grappling with the challenges of fast-paced growth. Indeed, race became the fulcrum for both assigning blame for the social ills that accompanied urban growth and for the consolidation of municipal power based on neighborhood politics. In the years following the 1917 riot, issues of racial contact in public places, in neighborhoods, and in the workplace remained front and center and came to define local politics. After 1917 the preoccupation with race inflected the geography of residence and employment, and the manipulation of racial tensions became a useful means for both politicians and industrialists to push through social change (or prevent it). Despite the dramatic changes brought about by two wars and an economic depression in the first half of the twentieth century, the fixation with race did not wane. Indeed, it intensified and set the strategic tone for the subsequent development of the city and its suburbs.

Race and Small-Town Life

Chester's backwater status on the eve of World War I had been centuries in the making. Pennsylvania's oldest city, Chester was first settled by Swedes and Finns as Upland in the 1640s. English settlers arrived seven years later. William Penn spent 1682 there with the intention of making Chester the colonial capital. A land dispute forced Penn to relocate up the Delaware River to present-day Philadelphia, leaving Chester to spend nearly two centuries as "an insignificant provincial hamlet."[3] Chester was the administrative center for county politics, serving as county seat in the first half of the nineteenth century. A borough until 1866, it was incorporated as a Pennsylvania third-class city in 1889 and elected a Quaker as its first mayor. The region's wealthy landowners and business families built stately homes on the city's north side, while the waterfront housed a few lumber mills and small shipbuilding companies.

Industry slowly began to exploit Chester's riverfront location around the time of the Civil War. A number of textile factories, including the massive Crozer mills, joined the city's oldest industrial firm, American Dyewood, which manufactured dyes for silk, wool, furs, and leather. Access to the Delaware River attracted the shipbuilding business in the 1850s. The expansion of industry and immigration, fast paced in other, larger cities in the late nineteenth century, occurred slowly and modestly in Chester. In the last few decades of the century, steel casting firms set up shop, manufacturing castings used in shipbuilding, dredging, cement and rolling mills, and hydraulic presses. New banks, department stores, theaters, and restaurants gave rise to the city's central business district. Between 1890 and 1900 Chester's population grew from just over twenty thousand to thirty-four thousand. Chester's leaders and its upstanding citizens may well have thought of their city as a more cosmopolitan version of a small town, but its reputation among outsiders had long centered on its notoriety as a freewheeling destination for vices such as drugs and alcohol, numbers rackets and gambling, and prostitution. Decades prior to the vast changes brought by World War I, Chester was widely known as Greater Philadelphia's "saloon town."

Overseeing and profiting from Chester's hybrid mix of industry and vice was the city's Republican political machine, which came to dominate local politics in 1875 and completed its political control over all of Delaware County by the start of World War II. Both the machine and its leadership are noteworthy for their longevity. John J. McClure took over as political boss from his father in 1907 and oversaw the machine's operations until his death in 1965. With the exception of 1904–1906, machine politics ruled Chester continuously for nearly a century. A nonmachine mayor was not elected until 1992.

Like most turn-of-the-century political machines, the base of McClure's power was liquor. The McClures first influenced and then controlled local- and county-level elected officials receptive to (and increasingly dependent on) the city's liquor licensing and saloon trade through the family's monopoly of wholesale liquor distribution. Chester and Delaware County's patronage system was a quid pro quo between tavern and saloon owners and elected officials: judges issued liquor licenses, and in turn bar owners drummed up votes and provided beer and a free lunch to voters on Election Day. Over time the machine deepened its reach into the everyday lives of Chester residents, granting favors in exchange for votes and strongly influencing a whole range of opportunities from their jobs and promotions to where they were welcome to live and the quality of the schools their children attended. The McClure machine handpicked candidates for county, city council, mayoral, and school board elections. The spoils of his rising political and economic power gave John J. McClure access to seats on the boards of banks, industrial firms, and other social and business interests. With his high-profile reputation, he found ardent support among local large manufacturing concerns, small business owners, and the growing legions of industrial workers. From time to time antivice social reform candidates surfaced to battle county and municipal corruption and to unseat elected officials who openly participated in and benefited from the machine-sponsored vice trade. But such efforts at reform and law and order were short-lived and produced no lasting changes to McClure's stranglehold on local politics. By the early 1900s McClure's machine was firmly in control of the politics and economy of Chester.[4]

McClure perfected his loyalty and patronage system through a multilayered network of political operatives who reached down deeply and bestowed favors to individual households. McClure locked up the votes in the five most populous and poorest wards, appointing ward lieutenants who wielded minor power over everyday affairs in their precincts but deferred to the machine boss over matters of significance. The vast network of machine operatives took orders from a storefront at Third and Kerlin Streets in Chester's South Ward known as "the Corner," where high-level Republican Party officials rubbed shoulders with their precinct-level counterparts. From there McClure consolidated his power over the political geography of the city (and soon after, Delaware County).[5] McClure also took advantage of the city's racial geography, defined by stable, unchanging, and seemingly ordinary social and spatial divisions between blacks and whites. Because the machine extended its vote-generating and favor-granting apparatus to all neighborhoods regardless of race, McClure countered periodic challenges to party rule from white progressives by mobilizing working-class districts, both black and white. McClure also found race a reliable and strategic means to effectively cover his involvement in the machine's lucrative side industries, including vice. In short, Chester's somewhat unremarkable black-white divide was vital to the success of the machine, and McClure spent considerable time and energy on maintaining it.

Like many other small northern cities, Chester's geography was a mix of white and black middle- and working-class neighborhoods of varied sizes whose boundaries changed imperceptibly over the decades. By 1900 Chester's black community had been established for well over a century, and the black population of forty-four hundred fluctuated very little prior to World War I. Although small in comparison to cities such as nearby Philadelphia, the community's economic and social lives flourished. A 1910 survey by the Pennsylvania Negro Business Directory lists six groceries, eight restaurants, two hotels, pool halls, barbershops, general contractors, cab operators, dressmaking shops, undertakers, and two black newspapers. There were nine black churches, with St. Daniel's Methodist, Asbury African Methodist Episcopal (AME), Calvary Baptist, Bethany Baptist, and Murphy AME Churches claiming the largest congregations. The Elks, Grand Order of Odd Fellows, Knights of Pythias, Masonic Lodge, and smaller fraternal orders, lodges, and social clubs recruited members from the working and middle classes. A neighborhood's location, character, and amenities reflected the prevailing social class of its residents, defined by occupation, income, and social status. Black small business owners, schoolteachers, ministers, physicians, and lawyers lived in the West End, the residential blocks close to the central business district. Black laborers, janitors, domestics, and saloon operators lived in the crowded blocks of the Eighth and Ninth Wards close to the industrial waterfront. Others employed in the city's thriving vice economy lived in Chester's "red light" district, Bethel Court, along with poor newcomers trickling (and later flowing) in from the South. Although separated from white residences, blacks were not confined or strictly segregated within a single area of the city. Instead, the number of small black neighborhoods, whose boundaries were neither rigidly fixed nor policed, expanded or contracted by a block or two depending on industrial hiring booms and busts.[6]

Regardless of a black neighborhood's location or the social class status of its residents, many of the everyday operations and the lives of those who lived there were overseen by a network of Republican political machine operatives or lieutenants. In addition to collecting protection fees and assuring voter turnout, McClure operatives mediated disputes among residents; raised bail money and legal fees for constituents in trouble; offered small sums of money, shelter, and other charitable resources to the needy; and supported local events, parades, and sports teams. Their activities and influence were not limited to the livelihoods of just the black working class. The machine controlled the limited professional occupational opportunities available to Chester's black middle class. McClure himself handpicked candidates for the school board and controlled the hiring of schoolteachers, the foremost career path to the middle class. Faced with no viable alternatives, blacks supported McClure and consistently voted for machine candidates. More than a handful profited from the association and gladly carried out the machine's bidding. As McClure intended, the machine held sway over the everyday lives of Chester's blacks, whether they resided in Bethel Court or on a modest middle-class residential street. Owners of funeral parlors, pool halls, hotels, and pharmacies that catered to a black clientele owed fealty to the political machine in one form or another. Chester's soft racial segregation was a normalized feature of everyday urban life, but what mattered was the political purpose that the racial divide served in assuring the dominance of the local political machine.

The network of black saloon keepers, shop owners, and hotel owners assured the necessary Republican votes on Election Days and the Republican machine in turn provided favors to locals ranging from jobs, school placements, legal assistance, and emergency aid. They were expected to faithfully contribute to campaigns and produce large election majorities for the machine—and they did. To the chagrin of

Chester's black residents, many of the very same political operatives who managed prostitution, gambling, and other vices on behalf of McClure played a hand in determining who obtained and maintained a black middle-class professional status. For the machine, the social (and to some degree physical) distance between the city's white and black residents allowed for a politically expedient and profitable manipulation of appearances. Black operatives were the visible "front men" on display and seemingly in control of the everyday operations of saloons, brothels, gambling joints, and flophouses, leaving white political leaders to profit outside the public eye.

The selective incorporation of blacks, on whites' terms, into machine politics was not unique to Chester. In the first two decades of the twentieth century, such incorporation was widespread in cities such as New Haven, Philadelphia, Cincinnati, Baltimore, and New York.[7] In most cases, this avenue of black entry into urban politics created the opening for autonomous black political leadership and organization commensurate with the waning influence of urban political machines. The power of Chester's political machine remained uncontested well into the final decades of the twentieth century, however, short-circuiting the development of black political autonomy.

Race and the Rapid Growth of the City

Chester's early twentieth-century racial compact proved functional to the local political machine, both maintaining the racial social and spatial status quo and solidifying the local power structure of the Republican Party. But Chester's rapid growth in wartime industrial workers upended this racial arrangement. Preparations leading up to the U.S. entry into World War I transformed Chester into an industrial boomtown almost overnight. Blame for the subsequent strain on the small city's resources coupled with increased patronage of its reputed vice district fell squarely on the shoulders of blacks, both newcomers and existing residents. The racial tensions that violently erupted in the summer of 1917 were not unique to Chester but reflected rising hostility among whites in many northern cities toward the influx of southern black workers. But the ease with which Chester's whites readily blamed blacks for social problems, including machine-run vice, speaks to the power of McClure's manipulation of racial divisions.

War demands for munitions and supplies brought a quick expansion of shipbuilding docks, assembly plants, and heavy industry along the waterfront and unprecedented growth in industrial employment. Only two years after it opened in 1916, the Sun Shipbuilding and Dry Dock Company (also known as Sun Ship) became the city's largest employer with over sixteen thousand workers manufacturing ships and repairing engines and machine parts. Other giants in Chester's industrial history— Baldwin Locomotive Works, Chester (later Scott) Paper, Westinghouse, and Sun Oil in nearby Marcus Hook—were founded during this time of extraordinary expansion. Tens of thousands of workers poured into Chester daily. Fifty-six local trains shuttled commuters back and forth from factories to their homes in Philadelphia, Wilmington, and adjacent small towns. But the most notable change was the staggering increase in new residents. Estimates at the time put the population growth rate at 100 percent, doubling the city's size from forty thousand in 1914 to eighty thousand in 1918.[8] Immigrants from Italy, Poland, Lithuania, and other parts of eastern Europe flooded the city, carving out ethnic niches cheek by jowl in existing neighborhoods and suddenly infusing the small city with a cosmopolitan flair.[9]

Business and political leaders welcomed growth and the fortunes it brought. But the city's long-term residents and civic leaders viewed rapid growth as mostly negative, as Chester's small-town feel was soon vanquished by industrial growth and urban congestion. Within eighteen months, the city's population trebled with the influx of immigrants and southern blacks. Manufacturing employment reached record levels; housing was woefully overcrowded and in short supply; and an antiquated infrastructure of sewers, roads, and transport groaned under the weight of increasing commerce and activity. Sidewalks were overcome

View of Market Street from the railroad, November 28, 1922. Reproduced by permission of the Delaware County Historical Society, Pa.

by the onslaught of commuters, newcomers, and strangers, and trolley lines teemed with a mix of shipbuilders, welders, factory workers, businesspeople, and mothers with their children. New pupils crammed schoolrooms. The city's housing supply, meanwhile, grew by only thirteen hundred units. New arrivals looking for employment found limited housing choices. Hastily erected work camps that popped up adjacent to factories were filthy and overpopulated. Many single-family homes became makeshift rooming houses with closets and bed space rented to mostly male boarders. Like all boomtowns, Chester was unprepared for the dramatic social changes that accompanied speedy growth. But among the class, ethnic, and racial divisions fueled by the city's rapid change, racial divisions rose to the fore.

In 1910 Chester was home to six thousand blacks, who were roughly 15 percent of the city's total population. At the peak of the war boom, the city's black population was over twenty thousand, or 25 percent of the total.[10] In 1916 and especially in the spring of 1917 thousands of black workers (mostly young males) poured into the Philadelphia region, including Chester, as part of the Great Migration to the North during World War I.[11] New arrivals gravitated to the city's black neighborhoods but found the established working- and middle-class districts unwilling or unable to accommodate such large numbers. Bethel Court, already teeming with Chester's poorest blacks, provided the main option; others included racially segregated work camps set up by the larger waterfront employers. The camps housed over two thousand black workers. Thousands found residence as lodgers in rooming houses and private homes, as tenants in converted garages and warehouses in the industrial areas, or as squatters in abandoned buildings.[12]

Chester's uneasiness, frustration, and uncertainty with rapid growth and congestion found a single, common focus among whites in general and the white middle class in particular. They placed the blame for a host of social ills squarely on the influx of black workers from the South and the subsequent unraveling of the city's racial geography. Industry's recruitment and hiring of black migrants into the local labor market fueled racial antagonism in Chester, as it did in many other industrial cities.[13] Factory owners certainly welcomed the arrival of new workers, be they blacks from the South or foreign-born whites. Although jobs were plentiful thanks to the wartime economy, most working-class whites were outright hostile to the rising numbers of blacks in the workplace. Blacks, who had once been assigned to menial tasks in most industries, were for the first time working alongside white workers. Additionally, Chester's white workers were well aware of tensions over the employment of black workers in cities elsewhere in the North and in the Midwest.

Labor's conflict with industrial management led to a series of well-publicized strikes and work stoppages in which the hiring of blacks was seen as threatening to union gains. Black workers were collectively branded as would-be strikebreakers. The steel and meatpacking industries, for example, hired black workers to break highly publicized strikes in 1892, 1894, and 1904, fueling the racial animosity of white union workers across the country. Closer to home, labor riots broke out at a sugar refinery in nearby South Philadelphia when the management hired black workers to replace unionized strikers in March 1917. Reports of black workers hired as strikebreakers in Chicago, East Saint Louis, and other cities galvanized more far-reaching negative sentiments toward blacks among organized white labor. In the days following the race riot in Saint Louis in early July 1917, the local press drew parallels between the circumstances that led to violence in that city and those festering in Chester.

While the threat to labor mattered to many locals, white middle- and working-class anger over the influx of southern blacks crystallized around the proliferation of vice, the perceived collapse in civic order, and the spike in street and property crimes that accompanied the city's rapid growth. With the rise in its economic fortunes, Chester's notoriety as a city "where anything goes" was more conspicuous than ever, rankling social reformers, the local press, and middle-class citizens alike. As industry along its waterfront grew, so too did the number of taverns, beer joints, pool halls, brothels, hotels, and flophouses. By 1914 there were more saloons than police officers in Chester, or roughly 1 saloon per every 987 citizens.[14] In 1917 the regional popularity of Bethel Court exploded when army and navy officials banned enlisted men stationed in Philadelphia from frequenting that city's local brothels and similar "resorts." Commuter trains and buses shuttled military and civilian patrons to and from Chester day and night. More patrons brought more drunken behavior, noise and commotion, and pickpocketing and similar petty crimes to Bethel Court—all conducted with apparent impunity.[15]

Whites attributed the surge in public drunkenness and the openness of prostitution and petty street crimes directly to the rising presence of working-age black males in the city. Like their white counterparts, many black migrants surely frequented Bethel Court. Unlike whites, however, many were simply lodgers relegated to the dilapidated rooming houses

Cover of September 1926 edition of *Chester*, a monthly industrial newsletter. Vol. 1, no. 3. Reproduced by permission of the Delaware County Historical Society, Pa.

and second-story lodgings above the brothels, saloons, and gambling dens. Bethel Court had long been the focal point of repeated social reform campaigns and the public scorn of both middle-class whites and established black families. As McClure's front men, however, blacks appeared to Chester whites to be responsible for the evils of the city's chief vice district. The machine capitalized on this, paying lip service to social reform campaigns while lining its pockets with protection fees and kickbacks and the profits from liquor and beer sales. Hiding safely behind the cloak of black operators, the machine profited from Bethel Court's saloons, brothels, gambling joints, flophouses, and rooming houses that catered to low-skilled laborers, the itinerant, and the poor. For Chester's whites and local newspaper editors, however, blacks were "customers," not residents. Bethel Court and all its immoral, criminal, and scandalous affairs were perceived as "a distinctly black problem."[16]

The vast increase in workers also increased the likelihood of mundane public interactions between whites and blacks. Whites, for the most part, found this new development disconcerting. Their view of poor, mostly young, male southern blacks tested their racial assumptions formed from years of predictable interactions between middle- and working-class whites and the stable working-class and West End middle-class blacks. Charges of "black incivility" abounded in conversations and increasingly in print in local newspapers. Impolite behavior on a streetcar, for example, blossomed into a panic of black insolence and the deliberate intimidation of whites. Tales of belligerent blacks routinely accosting whites on public sidewalks circulated in the city's white barbershops, beauty salons, shops, and restaurants. Newspaper coverage further racialized the social problems brought about by wartime expansion, adding fuel to racial tensions. In the spring and early summer of 1917 the *Chester Times* featured several stories about black perpetrators and white victims, ranging from minor affronts on streetcars to purported kidnappings and late night break-ins. Interview quotes from whites spoke of threats by aggressive black men to the public well-being and the moral and physical safety of white women especially. By July

1917 newspaper editorials and public discourse among whites gelled into a seamless rant in which black newcomers were potential scab laborers, disrespectful and threatening toward whites, immoral and indecent, prone to illegal behavior, and allowed to commit crimes with impunity. Discontent carried over into the blame whites placed on municipal leaders who failed to control the situation.

The highly charged atmosphere culminated in a deadly four-day race riot. Late in the night on July 24, 1917, a young black man named Arthur Thomas, his female companion, and another black couple walked through a predominantly white neighborhood on the city's West End as they made their way home from an evening at a summer carnival. Thomas exchanged words with a white man named William McKinney. Words soon turned to fisticuffs, and McKinney was stabbed repeatedly in the ensuing scuffle and died shortly thereafter. News of the "cold-blooded murder" of a white man by a "black thug" spread throughout the city, and within an hour hundreds of whites milled about the scene of the stabbing demanding retribution. Thomas and his three companions were arrested early the next morning, but by day's end only Thomas remained in custody, the others having arranged bail. That evening an enraged mob of whites marauded through the streets of Chester's black neighborhoods, touching off violent street battles that continued for four days. The level of brutality was alarming, as newspaper accounts printed in the riot's aftermath clearly indicate: the torching of row houses with their black occupants trapped inside, hand-to-hand combat in the city's West End involving several hundred whites and blacks armed with knives and sticks, block-by-block gun battles, random beatings of unarmed blacks and sympathetic whites, and indiscriminate thrashings of black rail and trolley passengers. The *Chester Times* referred to the July 26 rampage as "a night of terror in the city." Early in the mayhem, Chester's mayor called forth additional state and local police officers, a mounted patrol, and national guardsmen to restore order, but by July 30 seven people had been killed, twenty-eight had suffered gunshot wounds, and hundreds had been treated at a hospital or were still hospitalized.[17]

The Hardening of the Racial Divide

In the days immediately following the riot, Chester's political machine kicked in with its usual efficiency to facilitate a return to normalcy. After their bail was posted by a black machine lieutenant who ran a saloon in Bethel Court, one of McClure's handpicked magistrates had released Thomas's three companions from jail. But McClure underestimated the rage of his white political opposition, including the editors at the *Chester Times*. The paper featured several stories about the Republican Party's ties to the city's vice district and its deep connections in the black community. Unsurprisingly, the efforts to place responsibility for the unrest on the machine did little to diminish the blame the public accorded to Chester's black residents, long-term and recent. Reporting indicated that a few weeks prior to the July riot, the same magistrate had released two black males arrested for accosting a white girl in a city park. Their bail had been posted by the same Bethel Court operative. The *Chester Times* published stories and editorials claiming that local police and courts officially tolerated Bethel Court's rising lawlessness as part of the quid pro quo with machine operatives who managed saloons. Vocal critics of the machine held municipal politicians culpable for the riot and for abetting black lawlessness in exchange for votes. An editorial in a Philadelphia newspaper put Chester's Republican Party at the center of blame:

> These riots are traceable directly to the system of gang politics which has given Chester an unenviable notoriety. . . . The flaming up of the mob spirit is due to the fact that machine politicians have corrupted and demoralized a large part of the negro element, giving to criminals protection in return for political service. The result is that negro lawbreakers have committed almost endless acts of crime against whites and against the public peace with virtual impunity, and have become defiant of all restraint. It was because of frequent demonstrations that the processes of justice against negro offenders had been paralyzed by political influence that there was created a sentiment for lawless vengeance. . . . Intelligent

citizens were aware that the minor judiciary was but an annex of the political machine. . . . This was the real inspiration of the "race riots." There
was prevalent among the whites a firm belief that negro criminals would
not be brought to justice because they delivered political support to the
machine.[18]

Within weeks of the riot, the mayor ordered the police to prohibit the
sale of alcohol to military personnel visiting Bethel Court. The magistrate who had set low bail amounts for black offenders was dismissed
from office. Progressive reformers were emboldened by the public outcry and challenged machine-picked candidates for local judgeships and
city council seats in the fall elections. The vote count was close. Machine
candidates prevailed but only because of the overwhelming turnout of
black voters in their favor.[19]

The machine, which for decades had managed and manipulated the
spaces and opportunities for racial interaction, appeared to have ignored
the Chester white community's mounting racial antipathy toward interacting with an increasing number of blacks. Instead, the machine chose
the short-term promise of more money and votes from an increasing
black population. With the riot of 1917, the machine's exploitation of the
racial division that it had long helped engineer seemed in danger of im-
ploding. It did not. Despite the damning criticism of Chester's politics,
the social problems that accompanied fast-paced urbanization became
effectively racialized. Blacks were the chief cause of the riot, albeit with
the help of a political machine unwilling to impose law and order to
uphold white privilege, thinly disguised in the aftermath of the riot as
"community standards." Racial division only hardened, offering new
possibilities for the Republican machine to maintain its power among
Chester's whites and blacks.

Chester's black population declined considerably as World War I
ended and industries scaled back to prewar levels of employment. Nonetheless, white hostility toward the "encroachment" of blacks in public
spaces, neighborhoods, schools, and workplaces not only lingered but

Neon sign atop Crosby St. substation of Philadelphia Electric Company, erected in 1926 and removed in 1973. Reproduced by permission of the Delaware County Historical Society, Pa.

toughened. The residential division of blacks and whites that had otherwise gone relatively unnoticed for decades was fully embraced by whites, who sought to formalize and expand it. Responding to this aversion were actors who held strong connections to the political machine and offered a set of spatial fixes to racial tensions amenable to whites. Local realtors, real estate boards, financial institutions, and title companies tendered restrictive housing covenants as a means for white property owners to solidify neighborhood boundaries. Used in existing city neighborhoods and in greater numbers of newer "first-ring" suburbs, covenants bound residents not to sell, lease, or otherwise convey their property to particular groups, including blacks. Covenants and other restrictive devices mollified whites' reactionary need to hunker down, protect their communities, and exclude blacks from neighborhoods and, importantly, schools.

On the other side of the racial divide, the local machine too offered a spatial fix in the form of segregation and the development of a black city within a city. In the immediate aftermath of the 1917 riot, the machine offered Chester's black residents something progressive reformers could not: protection and security in the face of uncertainty and hostility from whites. After the riot hundreds of black residents fled the city and did not return. Most stayed and turned to their black ward leaders, who readily delivered the political machine's promise of safekeeping. The promise was kept, garnering deeper loyalty to the Republican Party from a vulnerable population. The machine in turn imposed a harder form of racial segregation. Within a decade white and black ward leaders defined the boundaries of Chester's black community in the city's Ninth Ward in the West End, solidifying votes and loyalty to the machine and providing a machine-dominated infrastructure for economic sustainability and social organization of a black ghetto. West Third Street near the intersection with Flower Street became the main commercial boulevard, lined with beauty shops, restaurants, social clubs, bars, and restaurants catering exclusively to blacks or with segregated spaces in white-owned businesses, such as movie theaters. Class distinctions in black communities became more defined, with the social and economic statuses of the middle class tied ever more closely to the operation of the political machine.

McClure intensified his grip on key facets of black city life. He "kept a careful eye on virtually every facet of the Black community—schools, housing, law enforcement, recreation, plus certain jobs in industry. Moreover, if anything escaped his view, there were certain underlings to report to him."[20] Within the boundaries of the West End, social class mobility was directly dependent on individual or family connections to the political machine. In his study of black politics in Chester, Richard Harris describes the development of an oligarchy of ward lieutenants, religious ministers, and civil rights organizations that held sway over economic and social lives well into the 1950s. Machine lieutenants oversaw the hiring of all schoolteachers (a key middle-class occupation), and favoritism in factory positions and promotions was rampant. Harris claims that in 1945 two-thirds of Chester's black schoolteachers were relatives or close friends of the community's political families.[21]

Wielding a Race Strategy in Industrial Employment

The black and white division of residential space in Chester was mirrored in workplaces, particularly in the larger industrial concerns concentrated along the city's waterfront. Employment was fully segregated by race, with black workers relegated to low-skill and menial labor positions, such as janitorial work. But the racial division of labor had further implications for the relationship between McClure's Republican political machine and industrial leaders, especially the fiercely antiunion Pew family, owners of Sun Shipbuilding and, in nearby Marcus Hook, Sun Oil (later, Sunoco). As the city's economy lurched from depression to yet another wartime boom, the machine's favoritism and patronage systems remained pivotal in staffing the industrial labor force. The relationship between the political machine and big industry remained stable as long as each side benefited. Over the course of workers' unionization efforts in the 1930s and wartime mass hiring in the 1940s, the machine-industry relationship turned adversarial, with Chester's black workers routinely caught in the middle of a contested politics of labor.

In the early 1930s Chester's political machine enjoyed the full support of local industrialists, among them the Pews and the operators of the city's largest concerns—Baldwin Locomotive, Delaware River Steel, Atlantic Steel Castings, Delaware County National Bank, Westinghouse, and the Philadelphia Electric Company.[22] McClure was a state senator the first half of the decade, assuring that the area's industrial interests were voiced in the state's capital and maintaining a probusiness climate in Chester and surrounding Delaware County. In Chester McClure benefited from corporate support for the Republican Party, which allowed the machine to adeptly fuse the politics of residence with those of the workplace. Before elections, the machine dialed up its voter turn-out system, requiring patronage employees at Sun and other industries to recruit additional voters for polling day. As further evidence of the corporate-machine alliance, the Sun shipyard president John G. Pew called "mandatory meetings" of workers for machine-sponsored politi-cal rallies. Republican Party membership was a de facto prerequisite for employment at Sun.[23]

The value of long-standing ties between the city's industrial leaders and its political machine became obvious when McClure lost his state senate seat and other machine politicians were swept from power in the 1936 election. Media coverage of the party leader's ability to avoid im-prisonment following his conviction on federal corruption and extor-tion charges fed the public outcry over his protected status. McClure had even survived a senate measure to force his resignation in 1935 only to lose in the election the following year. Even in Chester the machine's vic-tory was marginal, as only the majority black Ninth Ward supported the Republican ticket in each of its precincts. Defeated, McClure retreated to Florida. The 1936 elections proved equally disappointing for the Pew family's interests. President Franklin D. Roosevelt, who instituted price controls on various commodities as part of his economic recovery agenda, was reelected. Pennsylvania's Democratic governor taxed large businesses to finance public relief programs.

The loss of county and state senate elections to Democrats worried the Pews and other corporate elites, who had benefited from the ma-chine's probusiness and low corporate tax policies. Faced with no ac-ceptable local Republican leader to replace the retired McClure, Pew traveled to Florida to convince him to return as Delaware County's Re-publican Party leader. Pew offered funding for future election campaigns and complete control over the hiring decisions for all positions at the Chester shipyard and the refinery in Marcus Hook. In effect, all jobs at Sun would become machine patronage positions. McClure accepted, and the ranks of loyal Republican voters swelled. In the 1937 elections

Republicans swept back into local offices, and in 1938 the McClure machine experienced its strongest voter turnout ever.[24]

The McClure-Pew patronage employment deal began to unravel as a consequence of New Deal labor policies and the ongoing pressures for unionization at the shipyard. In an early effort to stave off unionizing, in 1922 Pew set up his own General Yard Committee for employee-management relations, which lasted until 1933. In 1934 the Industrial Union of Marine and Shipyard Workers of America (IUMSWA), a union active in shipyards along the East Coast, launched a campaign to organize Sun employees. Two years later 25 percent of Sun's forty-two hundred employees were IUMSWA members. In December 1936 the IUMSWA called a strike, leading to a shutdown until non-IUMSWA employees "broke through the picket line and succeeded in entering the shipyard. In the ensuing riot many were injured, some seriously."[25] Pew refused to negotiate a settlement. Instead, he turned to McClure to help form an employer-sanctioned worker's organization named the Sun Ship Employees Association (SSEA).[26]

McClure relied on loyal non-IUMSWA workers to break the strike, circulating petitions in support of the SSEA as the workers' bargaining unit. Within two weeks, twenty-six hundred employees had signed the petitions, and Pew met with SSEA representatives and agreed to negotiate workers' terms and conditions. The IUMSWA complained of unfair company practices to the National Labor Relations Board (NLRB) and secured a consent election to determine which organization represented Sun workers. McClure designated one of his operatives at Sun to pressure employees to support the SSEA in the NLRB's consent election in 1937.[27] Of the ballots cast, 2,398 voted for the SSEA and 1,412 for the IUMSWA. After the election the SSEA appointed McClure's operative "chief investigator of grievances," permitting him to pre-interview applicants for yard positions to gauge their union sentiments and hinder promotion and advancement of pro-IUMSWA workers. McClure's operatives formed a "strong-arm squad," selecting "boys good with their fists" who could be called on if there was any trouble.[28] For its part, Sun allowed SSEA activities and meetings to take place at the yard and on company time, and it set aside a room in a yard building for SSEA business. On December 31, 1937 Sun and the SSEA signed a labor conditions contract in which the SSEA was recognized as the exclusive representative of all workers employed at the shipyard.[29]

The IUMSWA continued to set its sights on Sun Ship, Chester's largest employer, and its unaffiliated labor organization the SSEA. The IUMSWA's efforts were emboldened in 1942—curiously enough by McClure, who worried that the powerful IUMSWA would eventually prevail and transfer thousands of Sun workers from the Republican ranks to the Democratic Party, the party more closely affiliated with the labor movement. In the NLRB proceedings in 1942, McClure's operative who had helped form the SSEA testified against the Pews, providing a first-hand account of the company's direct role in intimidating workers and approving strong-arm tactics to assure workers' compliance. The historian John Morrison McLarnon III sums up the curious turnabout in the machine's relationship with Sun:

> There was no direct evidence that [the machine's operative] got involved in the unionization of the shipyard in an attempt to save the labor vote for the Republican Party, no proof that he was sent into the shipyard as an agent of the machine. Nor was there any direct evidence that [he] testified against the Pews . . . at the behest of John McClure. On the other hand, the McClure lieutenant not only seemed to be at the center of most of the shipyard's labor problems, but had gone out his way to "expose" the illegal labor practices of the Pews. Subsequently, McClure began paying him a regular weekly salary.[30]

As a result of the machine lieutenant's damaging testimony, the NLRB found that Sun engaged in unfair labor practices and recommended that the IUMSWA replace the SSEA as the bargaining representative for Sun employees.[31] The Pews ignored the ruling, prompting the NLRB to file suit in the Third Circuit Court of Appeals. The court ruled in favor of the Pews, citing inconsistencies in the testimony of NLRB witnesses. But the Pews rightly predicted that the NLRB would force a second consent vote pitting the IUMSWA against the company's bargaining unit and would win. On June 30, 1943 the IUMSWA defeated the SSEA by a narrow margin.[32] But before the Pews' defeat the company tried another tactic: playing up racial tensions to advance an outright conflict among the ship workers.

In the midst of the labor union tumult, Sun Ship's operations expanded. At the start of World War II the labor demands of local industry brought a flood of new workers, both black and white, to the city. The wartime labor force for industries along the waterfront soared to 100,000, in contrast with the highest prewar figure of 45,000. The Chester wartime boom was in full swing. Labor demands opened new areas of employment to black workers previously restricted to unskilled jobs.[33] In addition to a labor shortage, the hiring of black workers was advanced in 1941 by Roosevelt's Executive Order 8802, which prohibited government contractors, such as munitions manufacturers and navy shipbuilders, from employment discrimination based on race, color, or national origin.[34] Prior to 1941 Chester's industries abided by the unwritten but rigorously enforced "racial qualification for employment." Baldwin Locomotive Works had restricted blacks to foundry work, but during the war the company expanded black employment throughout the company with the exception of the machine shop, "where employees threatened to quit if Negroes were employed." A National Urban League report on black wartime employment found sizable proportions of blacks in several Chester industries, including Penn Steel Castings (36.3%), Crucible Steel Casting Company (50.0%), Chester Electric Steel Company (55.8%), and South Chester Tube Company (18.2%). Sun Shipbuilding employed the overall largest number of black workers, which at peak employment was 15,000 of a total workforce of 35,000.[35] During World War II Sun became the largest single shipyard in the world.[36]

Sun's large black workforce belied the company's reluctance to comply with Roosevelt's Executive Order. The Pews only embarked on the mass hiring of blacks to confound unionization efforts and to rebuke Mc-Clure for his lapse in loyalty to the very company that had resurrected his political career. Hiring a large number of black workers provided a temporary political fix for the company's dual problems of an encroaching Democratic union and an increasingly fickle Republican political machine. The Pews employed a race strategy that (barely) complied with Executive Order 8802 and subverted the organizing efforts of the IUM-SWA. In May 1942 the company announced a plan to open a fourth production yard that would employ blacks exclusively; seven months later, Sun Ship's Yard No. 4 opened. By June 1943, 6,500 of the approximately 15,000 black workers employed at Sun Ship worked in Yard No. 4.[37]

The national office of the National Association for the Advancement of Colored People (NAACP) quickly condemned Sun's Yard No. 4 as a violation of Executive Order 8802 and a clear setback for ongoing campaigns of racial integration in the workplace. Given that blacks and whites were already working together in three of the company's yards, the NAACP challenged the need for a separate all-black yard.[38] However, the vast majority of Chester's black population welcomed Yard No. 4. First, its opening meant that many more jobs were available and only to black workers. Second, although wartime production demands opened up some skilled positions, in the other Sun yards black workers were largely confined to unskilled jobs. Separate and unequal pay scales for whites and blacks were the norm. As a fully operational unit, Yard No. 4 hired blacks for the entire range of production positions. The company trained local black workers as welders, plumbers, and electricians. Pew also recruited graduates of black colleges in the South and from the federal Engineering, Science, and Management War Training Program operated by the Works Progress Administration.[39] For Chester's working-class blacks, Sun's vocational training, higher wages, and promotions offered a real chance for economic advancement in an otherwise openly discriminatory labor market.

Despite criticism of segregation at Sun, the opening of Yard No. 4 put Pew in compliance with the employment demands of Roosevelt's War

Labor Board. But Pew's purposes for Yard No. 4 were expressly local. The IUMSWA's platform called for improved conditions for black workers at Sun. But the superior workplace benefits existed only in Yard No. 4, as Pew intended. Given the well-publicized and innovative benefits the yard provided its employees, Pew expected loyalty from Chester's black community and support in his antiunion and antimachine efforts. Pew achieved some measure of success at both, as evidenced by Yard No. 4's record membership in the SSEA. In the NLRB's second consent election in 1943, 4,700 Yard No. 4 workers voted in favor of Pew's SSEA and 700 for the IUMSWA.[40] By contrast, the majority of black workers in the other yards stayed home on Election Day, fearing violence from angry white coworkers. The IUMSWA won the consent election by a slim margin: 12,835 votes for the IUMSWA to 11,922 for the SSEA.[41]

For Pew, support for Yard No. 4 in Chester's black community could potentially thwart the machine's lock on the local Republican Party. McClure's ongoing efforts to secure the favor of the IUMSWA and the labor vote at Sun undermined Pew's SSEA. In response, Pew publicly endorsed and financed a rival candidate to McClure's handpicked choice for the state senate in the Republican primary. The loyalty of Yard No. 4 workers to Pew's candidate proved no match for the machine's ability to procure a favorable voter turnout.

Pew's efforts failed, but Yard No. 4's black workers' support for the SSEA exacerbated existing tensions between white and black workers (regardless of black workers' support for the IUMSWA in the other yards).[42] As in similar labor standoffs around the country, Pew in effect used the existing black-white tensions to "divide and conquer" and weaken the efforts of organized labor. By escalating racial tensions, "a certain amount of employer-employee antagonism [was] diverted into intra-employee conflict."[43] Yard No. 4 had less effect on worsening tensions in Chester. McClure's political machine easily fended off a challenge from black shipyard workers and their families. If anything, Pew's efforts created a minor division within the black community partially along class lines between Sun workers and black machine lieutenants and small business owners. The consequences of Pew's racial maneuvering were short-lived. With the end of World War II, the number of Sun employees in all yards declined, and Yard No. 4 was closed.[44] While employment competition between black and white workers clearly exacerbated existing racial antagonism, Pew used Yard No. 4 to stoke the embers of racial divisions in the working class and gain economic benefits.

Race Matters

Prior to World War I and the accompanying (and overwhelming) growth in the city's industrial economy, black and white relations appeared of no great concern to the social dynamics of everyday life in Chester. Racial discrimination and inequalities were widespread and obvious but at the same time, normalized and subdued as a result of "McClurism." Rapid social changes abruptly upended the political machine's ability to manage racial divisions and benefit handsomely from them, unleashing the wrath of white privilege in the race riot of 1917. Race, as a consequence, became the defining factor in reshaping the geography and social life of the city. What can be learned from these instances when race becomes central? Race did not simply appear or percolate to the top of community and later, workplace concerns. Its centrality to spaces of both residence and employment was intentionally trumped up and aggravated to benefit the political machine and local industrialists.

The events depicted in this chapter point to the historical ascendance of a systematic and strategic manipulation of race for practical political and economic purposes. Black isolation and exclusion became utilitarian, a means to profit from urban development and control workplace conditions. Racial divisions became the preferred standard for dividing spaces and imbuing them with differing levels of economic and social value. Race, then, was intentionally chosen as the ordering mechanism for the development of the city and its suburbs.

3

How to Make a Ghetto

Throughout the years of World War II, Chester experienced a housing crisis. Thousands of black and white workers had crammed into the small city, drawn to employment in the waterfront's industrial war machine that built ships and churned out munitions day and night. In addition, demand for housing trebled when the war ended and the troops returned home, but only for a short while. By the late 1940s the pull of the suburbs reduced Chester's population, just as it did in similar cities in the Northeast and the Midwest. During this short-lived shift from too much housing demand to not enough, entire neighborhoods remained racially segregated. Suburbanization altered the realities of racial segregation, but only in its scale. Chester became smaller, poorer, and disproportionately black, and the towns and subdivisions of surrounding Delaware County became larger, wealthier, and overwhelmingly white.

This quick synopsis of the growth of the suburbs and the ensuing changes and challenges to Chester conforms to the established narrative of American postwar suburbanization and urban decline. In the second decade of the twenty-first century, this history is well-known, primarily because Americans still live with many of the postwar era's debilitating consequences for its older cities. Yet perhaps as a result of its repeated retelling, the detailed racial mechanics of this process have been lost, ignored, or glazed over at best. This chapter pulls apart the "postwar ghetto and suburbanization" narrative and focuses on the institutions and actors to investigate racial exclusion as a means for regulating the city and developing its suburban hinterlands. It examines the political and administrative coordination involved in pushing racial exclusion from the city to its suburbs. Together, these actions point toward the intentionality, not the inevitability, of suburban exclusion, that suburban development was a collective spatial fix for actors and institutions to both cope with and profit from the pressures of racial integration.

Underlying the rise of the ghetto and the suburb were deep concerns among whites to preserve the racial status quo and fight off threats to undo it. The collective fears of whites conformed to the dominant racial ideology of the time, but they were also strategically stoked by the localized race-baiting by actors and institutions with vested interests in urban and regional change. The chapter begins with the story of a failed effort in the 1940s to construct an all-black private market housing development in Chester called Day's Village. The Day's Village story reveals how a race-based strategy facilitated postwar urban segregation, the use of residential restrictive covenants, racial steering, and the other decisions and actions to prevent racial integration in both the city and its expanding suburbs. The chapter closes with two stories of racial violence in 1958 and 1963 in suburban Delaware County. Both stories bring to light not only the most appalling aspects of racial exclusion but also the degree to which entire communities bought into the production of the suburbs as a defensive spatial fix to the threat of racial integration.

Day's Village and the Complexities of Racial Segregation

For the first half of the twentieth century, Chester's fate was ruled by the industrial boom-bust cycle that regulated the city's economy, much of its social life, and the fluctuations in its population. By the time the city's industries geared up for a second war effort in the early 1940s, its housing stock bore evidence of past overcrowding followed by near abandonment in the Great Depression. The boom-bust economy clearly took its toll on the city's urban infrastructure. Indeed, there was no incentive to build new housing in the 1930s and the first half of the 1940s. Landlords simply raised rents and packed in more tenants during periods of high demand and during slowdowns allowed properties to age without repairs or upkeep.

As bad as the substandard housing conditions were for white residents, they were much worse for their black counterparts. Although Chester's black population grew in response to the recruitment of unskilled and semiskilled industrial workers from southern states, the spaces in the city designated as "Negro neighborhoods" following the 1917 riot remained the same size. In 1940 nearly 60 percent of the total black population resided in the city's Eighth and Ninth Wards. Most of the several thousands who relocated for work during the war stayed on as residents in these confined, segregated neighborhoods. Black communities were further divided by status, tenure, and social class, with the middle-class, longer-term residents maintaining homes in prized sections of neighborhoods and newcomers renting beds in flophouses or tripling up in small rooms in subdivided, aging, and decrepit homes.[1]

The dismal conditions of everyday life for blacks in Chester in the 1940s were spelled out in the *Survey of Race Relations and Negro Living Conditions in Delaware County* (1946), part of a report commissioned by the National Urban League. The survey labeled the housing shortage "serious" and found "practically no new homes for Negro occupants having been constructed in the county for nearly 20 years."[2] Half of the black population lived in antiquated dwellings without adequate sanitation, ventilation, or heat. The survey laid most of the blame on segregation. By the early 1940s wartime restrictions on new housing construction, growth in industrial employment, and unyielding racial segregation caused demand to far exceed Chester's limited and dated "black housing" supply. However, the possibility for a vast improvement in the bleak situation appeared on the horizon in 1942. First, the recently (1939) formed Chester Housing Authority (CHA) opened the 350-unit Lamokin Village in the Ninth Ward. Lamokin Village was not only the city's first public housing development, it was also its first segregated one, comprised entirely of black tenants. The opening of Lamokin Village eased demand for "black housing" somewhat (rather than build on an undeveloped parcel, the CHA razed 149 Ninth Ward homes, registering a net gain of 201 new housing units).[3]

A second promising remedy to the "black housing" crisis appeared the same year. The high-stakes real estate developer Joseph P. Day proposed an ambitious plan for newly constructed private market homes for Chester's black families. Day was a pioneer in large-scale real estate development. Based in New York City, he oversaw the development of thousands of housing units in cities in the Northeast. He began as an auctioneer, selling thousands of lots in Queens, New York, and the parcels later developed as Hunts Point in the Bronx. His early days as an auctioneer brought him to Camden, New Jersey, where he successfully sold hundreds of government-owned wartime housing units, and to Chester. In 1922 the U.S. Shipping Board Emergency Fleet Corporation contracted Day to auction 278 homes, 23 apartment buildings, and 75 vacant lots in Chester's thirty-five-acre Buckman Village. At the height of World War I, the Shipping Board had purchased land and developed Buckman Village to house shipbuilders and other industrial workers employed at Sun Shipbuilding and other industries along the waterfront. "When the war ended this activity stopped almost overnight," according to the *New York Times*, "and Chester entered into an industrial depression of great magnitude."[4]

In the twenty years after the Buckman Village auction, Day became a major developer, constructing large tracts of homes in Brooklyn, northern New Jersey, and Connecticut. He championed home ownership for average working-class Americans in the midst of the Great Depression and was an early advocate for the mass adoption of then-novel long-term residential housing mortgages. In 1942 Day returned to Chester at the height of its demand for housing, proposing 150 new homes for black families to be built on a tract of land abutting Highland Gardens, an all-white residential community. Day and a handful of other developers saw demand for (and profit in) black housing developments in northeastern cities experiencing an influx of wartime workers. Chester seemed ideal for the segregated project for blacks called Day's Village.

The plan for Day's Village met with immediate opposition from the residents of adjacent Highland Gardens and its chief financial underwriter, the Connecticut Life Insurance Company. The development of Highland Gardens was considered a feat for housing-poor Chester. The all-white community of seven hundred brand-new single-family, attached (row) houses opened in 1942, the same year Day proposed his project. Both Connecticut Life and the new residents claimed that the close proximity of Day's Village would threaten Highland Garden's property values. They argued that the proposed increase in residents would overburden local roads and water and sewer systems and over-stretch the capacities of neighborhood schools (which were all white). Day contended that the site was ideally situated for the size of the project he had in mind. Plans for the site complied with the specifications for Federal Housing Administration (FHA) insurance, and the project won the first rounds of FHA approval. In addition, Day received favorable purchase options on the land where Day's Village would be constructed. The owner of that property was Chester's Republican political boss McClure.[5]

In response to the complaints, the FHA proposed that Day build his project in an all-black neighborhood instead. Day declined, and the agency, under pressure, eventually backed down from its approval to underwrite the construction of Day's Village. Day's purchase option expired and the plan for modern housing for Chester's black families vanished. McClure quickly sold his property to the CHA to build a very different community—a segregated white public housing project called McCaffery Village.[6] In spite of civil rights achievements and significant federal and state antidiscrimination legislation that followed in the ensuing decades, McCaffery Village remarkably remained a solidly all-white community until the early 1970s.

Although it was never built, there is much to be gained from the story of Day's Village. The broad contours of the saga—white protests over an adjacent black community and fears of racial integration in schools—are clearly not exceptional, given the state of race relations in 1940s America. Yet as the following sections reveal, the Day's Village story demonstrates the unyielding intentionality in and commitment to racial exclusion in urban and regional development. The Day's Village dispute speaks to the complexities of segregation for the early civil rights movement, the importance of racial exclusion to private and public housing, and the significance of race strategies to the political economy of suburban development.

The Limits of Civil Rights Activism

The Day's Village saga illustrates the capricious political nature of racial exclusion not only as a strategy of uneven urban development but also as a focal point for resistance to it. First, Day's proposal and the resistance to it posed a quandary for Chester's progressive black leaders. Day's Village, after all, called for a segregated all-black community. Given its mandate in favor of racial integration this proposal was something the NAACP, the key national civil rights organization, found difficult and ultimately impossible to support. The prospect of an all-black community conformed to and upheld the expectations of racial segregation as defined and policed by whites. Yet in a twist, whites rejected Day's Village because its planned location outside "black space" threatened to upset existing racial boundaries, a prospect Chester's black civil rights community found appealing. Further, key parts of Chester's black community supported an all-black development but in a historically all-black area of the city. For many established black families and community leaders, the flip side of segregation had provided the chance for advancement in social class. This was true especially for those with connections to the local white power structure.

For George Raymond, who became president of the local chapter of the NAACP in 1942, the controversy over building Day's Village amounted to a serious challenge to the struggle against racial discrimination in Chester. Thousands of blacks worked in Chester's war industries but were denied decent housing and were relegated to racially segregated and overcrowded slums.[7] But Raymond found little support or traction for making Day's Village a high stakes issue either nationally or locally. Raymond focused on the objections to the project's proposed location, specifically the Highland Gardens residents' charges that blacks living nearby would lower their property values. He was convinced the FHA's decision to rescind approval for the project was the result of such charges, a claim the FHA denied. In his petition to the national NAACP, Raymond cited the FHA's decision as "flagrant evidence of bias."[8] But the NAACP viewed Day's Village, a segregated housing project, as incompatible with its ideological and practical goals of racial integration and chose not to take up the issue.[9]

The fact that Raymond found little traction for the Day's Village issue at the local level reveals the thornier dimensions of persistent spatial segregation and activist efforts to undo it. The residential separation of blacks and whites had clearly hardened over the decades since the 1917 riot; Chester was a fully segregated city in the 1940s. The city's busy retail and entertainment district barely tolerated black customers by providing separate services or banned them altogether. Its central hospital maintained different wards for white and black patients. White and black students attended separate public schools until the ninth grade.[10] The scale and longevity of hardened segregation inevitably produced a separate and viable community life. Middle- and working-class black neighborhoods matured as communities, with churches and civic organizations and black-owned shops, restaurants, bars, and funeral homes. As chapter 2 pointed out, Chester's white elites and government leaders actively fostered a dependent black leadership, bestowing various favors, political appointments, and a share of often ill-gained cash. Black political incorporation was a strategic and highly useful tactic. The spatial politics of the ward system nurtured the "cooperation" of black leaders (and a large part of the middle class). "Chester's native-born blacks knew their place," writes the Delaware County historian McLarnon. "Most accepted the fact that Chester was a segregated city, with all that such segregation implied."[11]

For Chester's blacks, segregation was both unfair and compulsory; their acquiescence or acceptance of it as a fait accompli mattered little. What mattered was that segregation had seeped fully into the dimen-

sions of everyday life, providing countless collective and personal obstacles and some opportunities. The reality of segregation provided a
degree of certainty, especially following the violence of 1917. A change
in the status quo was much desired, but improvement in housing opportunities and social reform was far from guaranteed. As head of the
NAACP, Raymond was fully aware of the skepticism and fear of change
in the black community. More importantly, he knew Chester's white
elites had set down the unwritten rules for black acquiescence and compliance and enforced them through carrot-and-stick favors and retribu-
tions. But Raymond understood that a radical change in local politics
was essential for social change.

After Day's Village, Raymond spent the next half decade tackling
Chester's segregation head-on. In 1945 he put together an all-black reform ticket for the city council, magistrate, and school board elections
that ran on a platform for improving working-class housing, schools,
police services, and support for black businesses.[12] The ticket was hand-
ily defeated by the candidates the white political machine sponsored,
especially in the black precincts. After a similar failed effort in 1947, Raymond abandoned his elections strategy. Chester was a closed society and
the way to move forward was to acknowledge the resilience of the local
political machine and work within and, to the degree possible, around
it.[13] To the dismay of a small but ardent group of reformists, Raymond
adopted a gradualist approach to civil rights in line with the local mod-
erate Old Guard led by self-professed "practical-minded" church leaders. Key among these was the Reverend J. Pius Barbour, a respected elder
in the black community who was a mentor to the young Martin Luther
King Jr. when he was a student at Chester's Crozer Theological Seminary.[14] Barbour advised Raymond to act measuredly and patiently and
to focus on long-range goals. Raymond had greater success in fighting
discriminatory practices in public and commercial spaces than in his efforts to combat housing discrimination and residential segregation. His
achievements included the eventual end of segregated accommodations
in restaurants, theaters, and hotels..

The Unyielding Commitment to Racial Segregation

For Chester's whites, Day's Village threatened to upend the spatial compact that formed the basis of the city's full-on black-white divide and the range of social, cultural, and economic privileges that came with it. Whites had grown accustomed to such privileges accorded by a segregated city policed and micromanaged by their local Republican political leaders. To them, Day's Village was yet another possible encroachment of their turf by blacks and an added reminder of the city's demographic changes, the threat to the status quo, and the emerging possibilities opening up in the suburbs. In this instance, the Day's Village story is instructive to an understanding of how the city's power holders played into the white community's fear of racial integration to shape the political and economic contours of urban and suburban development.

Day's Village was the largest but not the first proposed private residential development that threatened the status quo of racial physical segregation. But such threats were few and successful threats exceptional. After the 1917 riot whites in Chester felt compelled to maintain, by lawful and unlawful means sanctioned by city leaders, the boundaries between white and black communities. Residential restrictive covenants dated back to the early 1920s. They increased after 1926, when the U.S. Supreme Court validated their use to prohibit individuals from specific racial, ethnic, and religious groups from living in certain neighborhoods. Racial covenants in neighborhoods such as Highland Gardens were enforced by unwritten arrangements between builders, realtors, the city's building and permits department, and political ward leaders. Local banks rarely approved residential loans without such restrictions implied in the sale contract. The National Urban League's 1946 study of racial conditions in Chester and Delaware County noted that Chester's "system of unwritten restrictive covenants" was a highly effective means of preventing blacks from renting or purchasing homes except in certain designated areas (namely the Eighth and Ninth Wards).[15] Although the Supreme Court overturned its decision on covenants in 1948, the new ruling applied only to the enforcement of deed restrictions. Secretive covenants between buyers and sellers remained common.[16]

Exclusionary efforts redoubled as the increase in the numbers of black industrial workers stretched the occupancy of neighborhoods and brought on demands for new housing. Given the power of Republican ward politics, local white control over the spatial allocation of private housing proved manageable and predictable. The machine oversaw building permits and the inspections process, enforced zoning ordinances, and held considerable sway over the practices of banks and other lending institutions. According to the Urban League's study, private landowners actively blocked plans by home builders to construct new housing for blacks in undeveloped spaces, even on the fringe of the city. The "self-administration" of blacks in specific electoral wards by machine-sanctioned black leaders kept "troublemakers" and any plausible threats to the spatial status quo in check.

Yet Chester's racial status quo seemed vulnerable to "external" developments on the horizon. The nation's turn toward government-sanctioned, subsidized housing posed conceivable problems for the persistence of the city's segregation in its current form. Public housing policies pertaining to financing, site location, and tenant selection were written at the state and federal levels, beyond direct local political influence. Federal housing policy generally addressed a national housing crisis and reflected progressive interests in solving problems of housing affordability. The local NAACP saw the promise of federal housing policy as an external and therefore progressive means to alter the city's built environment and combat racial segregation.

The promise of relief from housing segregation was short-lived. Federal housing policy was ultimately administered with considerable autonomy by local public housing authorities. From the onset, the McClure machine folded the newly available opportunities provided by federal public housing financing into the patronage operations of the machine, including rewarding loyal operatives with seats on the Chester Housing Authority (CHA) board, which chose site locations for proj-

ects, awarded contracts for the construction of projects and their maintenance, and most importantly, oversaw tenant selection.[17] Before the
first bricks were laid and the mortar dried, the machine compelled black
ward leaders to buy into plans for fully segregated public housing projects (or face the option of none at all).[18] The all-black Lamokin Village
was completed in 1942 and one year later the CHA opened two all-white
projects, McCaffery Village (350 units) and William Penn Homes (300
units), in the city's Seventh Ward. The CHA's tenant selection office enforced a strict policy of racial segregation in all three projects.[19]

Despite vast changes in national urban policy after the war, Chester's
public housing situation changed very little. The city government readily
dealt with any potential policy threat to segregation. In 1946, for example,
local housing authorities who administered federal policies adopted income criteria for the selection of tenants of "low-income" government-
subsidized projects across the United States. The CHA began to enforce
the income ceiling policy in June 1947, issuing lease termination notices
to now-ineligible tenants in the all-black Lamokin Village and the all-
white William Penn Homes and McCaffery Village. The vast majority
of the war workers housed at McCaffery and Penn earned incomes well
above the low-income eligibility criteria. The CHA estimated that 60 percent of the residents of all three projects were ineligible under the new income ceiling policy; Lamokin Village had the smallest share of ineligible
residents, with 166 of 350 units to be made available there.[20] The purpose
of the new federal policy was to free up housing units for low-income
families. The expectation was that as families with incomes too high to
remain in public housing departed on their own accord or were evicted,
more units would be made available to needy low-income residents.

Given Chester's demographics in the late 1940s, the majority of the
city's low-income families were black. That fact coupled with the discriminatory practices of private housing landlords meant that the demand for housing among low-income blacks was exorbitantly high.
Seeing an opportunity for racial integration, Raymond publicly pressed
the CHA to enforce the federal policy and rent the vacated McCaffery

and Penn units to income-eligible blacks.[21] Instead, the CHA maintained its practice of tenant segregation while complying with the new policy. In 1948 the number of vacant public housing units increased due to evictions, but the CHA intentionally left the units vacant. The CHA chose to maintain the segregation status quo; no blacks were housed in either Penn or McCaffery.[22]

Chester's white leadership remained committed to preserving the racial status quo at considerable expense to the housing concerns of its citizens. The U.S. Supreme Court's 1948 decision striking down restrictive covenants in private housing had only a negligible effect on racial segregation, given the political machine's direct and indirect control of the housing market. It did, nonetheless, spell the end of racial segregation in public housing. As pressures from Washington, D.C., Harrisburg, Pennsylvania, and Raymond's NAACP mounted, the CHA begrudgingly took initial steps to integrate over a period of three years. Pennsylvania's governor eventually intervened, replacing the chairperson of the CHA with a nonmachine Democrat who favored desegregating public housing. In December 1955 the CHA finally passed a resolution formally abolishing segregation in all Chester public housing projects. The action was partly due to Democratic control of the CHA board and partly due to threats by the NAACP to sue the city for violation of the Pennsylvania Housing Authorities Law. According to the CHA resolution, vacant units were to be allocated on the basis of need and income eligibility, not "race, religion, color or creed."[23] William Penn Homes was integrated over a one-year period. The CHA's Democratic chairperson noted, "Despite the ill-informed and inconsiderate pressures upon us by those who fear any change, I for one, am glad we decided as we did." He went on to say that desegregation was a "harbinger of things to come at a time of difficult, but necessary, historical adjustment."[24] But he was overly optimistic. Shortly after the resolution passed, the Republicans successfully ousted him.[25]

The announcement of integration plans for McCaffery Village met with quick opposition. The Republican city council members balked, claiming that the timing for further integration was unsuitable and, as the Republican John Nacrelli, future mayor of Chester, proclaimed, the area was "not yet ready to accept it."[26] When Raymond threatened another lawsuit, the CHA agreed to rent to three black families. The reaction of white residents was swift and violent—two of the homes were vandalized and CHA officials were threatened. According to McLarnon, when the new CHA director asked the mayor for police protection, "the mayor refused, claiming that the less publicity the situation received, the sooner tensions would ease. Absent aggressive support from city authorities, few blacks were willing to risk the move."[27]

In clear evidence of the resilience of racial exclusion, Chester's public housing remained segregated long after the announced end of the CHA's formal discriminatory tenant placement policies. As noted earlier, McCaffery Village remained occupied exclusively by whites into the 1970s, while two other projects, Lamokin Village and Ruth L. Bennett Homes (built in 1952) housed blacks exclusively. William Penn Homes was officially integrated, but a vast majority of tenants were black. In May 1972 the Pennsylvania Human Relations Commission ordered the CHA to "racially integrate its four older public housing projects, directing that tenant selection policies must result in occupancy that reflected the white-black ratio in all projects combined—80% black and 20% white."[28] The commission's insistence that the city's housing authority enforce a policy that was two decades old met with little resistance. By 1970 Chester's white population was barely over half the size it had been in 1950.

Expanding the Scale of the Racial Divide

Even Chester, with its sophisticated apparatus of racial segregation, faced the inevitability of racial progress stemming from demographic changes, the achievements won by civil rights activism, and progressive federal legislation. But the status quo would not go away without a long fight and ultimately a well-developed strategy for whites to abandon the city coupled with an equally calculated scheme to exclude blacks from the growing suburbs. Whites won the battle over Day's Village, and government agencies, realtors, and banks actively policed the segregated private housing market. White-controlled institutions such as the CHA kept the integration of public housing at bay far longer than Raymond could have thought possible. Indeed, in retrospect the longevity of segregation in Chester seems remarkable. And it is telling that its longevity was due to the diligent enforcement by individuals and institutions and not simply a consequence of changing market conditions that favored suburbanization. Such diligence became the norm throughout the rest of Delaware County. Suburbanization was but the active reproduction of the black-white divide on a larger scale, requiring a significant amount of energy to enact a more expansive racial order. At the heart of it, mass postwar suburbanization was a spatial fix for the eventual upending of the racial status quo in the city.

On its surface, the suburbanization of Delaware County was similar to that of most northeastern cities between 1900 and 1960. As in most metropolitan regions, city growth and suburbanization first occurred in tandem in the early decades of the twentieth century. Wealthier and middle-class whites began to leave Chester in sizable numbers after 1920. Between 1920 and 1940 the city's white population decreased from 51,000 to 49,000. The downward trend was partially reversed between 1940 and 1950 as a result of the war industry and the return of veterans after 1945. First-ring suburbs grew quickly. The townships of Darby and Ridley, adjacent to Chester, were the first to show rapid growth in the number of lower-middle-class and working-class whites. Glenolden's population rose from 1,944 in 1920 to 5,452 in 1950, and Sharon Hill's population rose from 1,780 in 1920 to 5,465 in 1950. The populations of Ridley Park, Norwood, and Prospect Park more than doubled between 1920 and 1950. All these communities were primarily residential towns with some remaining farms, little commerce, and with few exceptions, no industry. Trains and then automobiles shuttled workers to and from their city jobs.[29] In the 1950s white out-migration picked up pace and continued unabated for two decades.[30] Between 1940 and 1960

Chester and suburbs of Delaware County.

the population of Delaware County increased by 250,000 persons, many of them working-class whites who left Philadelphia neighborhoods. By 1960 eight of every nine persons in Delaware County lived outside Chester.[31] Meanwhile, in Chester between 1950 and 1960 the white population decreased by 18.8 percent, while the black population increased by 53.4 percent.[32]

The demographics of suburbanization—the changing racial and class geography of a metropolitan region—are informative, but they do not in themselves explain or shed much light on how and why regional changes occurred the way they did. To adequately address questions of how and why, we need to focus on racial exclusion as the key political and economic strategy driving urban and suburban development. Racial segregation shifted in scale, moving from spatial divisions within the city to divisions between the city and its suburbs. The geographic expansion of racial exclusion, so to speak, is the deliberate outcome of decisions by actors and institutions. Chester, already formed by a half century of hardened segregation, provided the political base or locus for suburban racial exclusion. The growth of the suburbs was less an abandonment of the city than an expansion in spatial scale of racial division.

The local politics of suburbanization strategically stoked and harnessed the racial fears and anxiety of whites across the class spectrum. As discussed above, Chester's middle- and working-class whites were accustomed to a segregated city and fought hard to maintain it as such. Although the arising affordability of the suburbs was a pull to larger numbers of white residents (especially with the Serviceman's Readjustment Act of 1944 or GI Bill), many clung to their city homes and familiar neighborhoods. The racial boundary lines between residential neighborhoods were increasingly put to the test, but they were also enforced and policed largely through intimidation and violence directed at black newcomers. As late as 1960 the local NAACP registered its concerns about the increasing instances of violent retribution by whites toward black newcomers on their blocks.[33]

In his book-length memoir the Chester native and *New York Times* columnist Brent Staples recalls his childhood in what was still a predominantly Polish and Ukrainian neighborhood on Second Street near Highland Avenue in the late 1950s. He tells of flying a wooden plane propelled by a rubber band that landed in the backyard garden of a Ukrainian family. The elderly white home owner snatched the plane, split it into several pieces, and returned it to Staples. "A beautiful plane had been reduced to splinters by a grandfather. Grandfathers were supposed to be nice, especially to children. I suspect that grandpa missed the days when black people were confined to small streets and alleys near the river; when the shipyard and the oil refineries were segregated, complete with supervisors for the colored; when the Poles and Ukrainians lived alone with their own, their schools, and their bakeries. Now black people were right next door. Grandpa needed someone to look down on."[34] Staples mentions the white strongholds of Highland Gardens and McCaffery Village in particular. "We knew instinctively not to detour as we came and went from school," he wrote. "Keep to Highland Avenue: the message was delivered to us on the air."[35] As Staples's memoir attests, the process of white flight was neither quick nor readily accepted. In Chester and similar cities whites clung to a dying racial order in part because many believed white institutions and politicians would step in and rescue them.

Chester's well-managed political machine had provided the underlying institutional framework for the city's entrenched segregation, mustering the powers of the housing authority, the police force, and the electoral ward system fueled by patronage. But the political machine also stoked the embers of racial integration and therefore, conflict. It was, after all, the Republican boss McClure who tendered the sale of the land adjacent to Highland Gardens to Day to build an all-black community, setting off a furor among his white constituency. McClure's decision may seem surprising, but in the larger context of the politics of urban development, his tug on the seams of the very divisions he helped design and maintain makes perfect sense.

The political infrastructure that led to the eventual city-suburb racial divide was put in place by the outward expansion of the local political machine. As early as the 1920s McClure's Republican machine realized the potential and the urgency of bringing the growing towns and villages of Delaware County under its control.[36] The ability to acquire political control of the nascent suburbs required the skilled management and governance of Chester, a feat fully accomplished by the 1940s. For decades Chester police officers, for example, were election "poll workers," reminding black and white voters to cast their ballots for Republican candidates while wearing their service uniforms.[37] Following the elections, patronage jobs were (re)allocated to ward leaders according to voter turnout numbers.[38] Many of these individuals, their families, and their social networks could be called on for similar "party work" in the suburban expanse.

The established political power base in Chester easily allowed the machine to extend its governance to the entire county.[39] Chester's Republican machine found little political resistance to its rapid expansion in the suburbs. The Republican Party dominated the growth of the Greater Philadelphia region (to the north of Chester), especially in nearby Montgomery County.[40] In his discussion of Republican politics in Delaware County, McLarnon points to the Chester organization's high degree of organization and party discipline in the nascent suburbs: "The foundation of the organizational structure was the party's cadre of committee people—one man and one woman from each of the county's 250 precincts, chosen at the primary election in even-numbered years. The committee people constituted the standing army of the machine. Each maintained continual oversight over his or her domain, paying particular attention to new arrivals in the precinct. When a family moved in, the committee person made the first political contact, insuring that the new neighbors understood the lay of the political landscape."[41] To help simplify expansion and control, McClure founded an informal executive committee, the Delaware County Republican Board of Supervisors, comprised of prominent local bosses charged with overseeing political affairs in designated regions in the county.[42] As McLarnon argues, the genius of what was commonly known as the "War Board" was its ability to pander to the needs and concerns of each region of the county, including Chester. This facilitated an emerging racial divide between city and suburb, with Chester's political operatives (including black ward leaders) playing to increasing demands for racial inclusion and integration in the city and their suburban counterparts reassuring home owners of their long-term investment in a white community. In one of the more striking examples of race-baiting, McLarnon tells of the 1961 countywide election in which the Republican Board of Supervisors in suburban Springfield had black party workers from Chester pose as potential Democratic home buyers, stoking white voters' fears (and turnout).[43]

Chester's political machine laid the systematic framework for whites to exit Chester and to avail themselves of residential opportunities and the security of an intact racial order, which were both available in nearby suburban towns and villages. As whites moved into newer housing in the small towns that dotted Delaware County, they often held onto their Chester properties, dividing them into rooming houses or apartments for black tenants with the consent of the McClure machine. The expansion of the city's black neighborhoods did not occur willy-nilly; it too was politically managed. Unlike in larger cities, blockbusting—the sale of homes in white neighborhoods to blacks to encourage panic selling among whites—was finely coordinated and managed. Both black and white political ward leaders communicated and worked with realtors and home sellers in overseeing racial changes block by block. All the while, the political machine conveyed mixed messages regarding Chester's prospects at integration or continued segregation. As demographic pressures and more progressive national efforts at integration evolved over time, so did the machine's ambiguity regarding racial changes in the city. It is also important to note that the machine's reach into the suburbs did not mark an abandonment of its hold over Chester. The machine kept its control over an increasingly black city well in place. As indicated, the expansion of Chester's political control over Delaware County and its racial landscape was only made possible by the successful control of Chester, including the continued domination of the city's black wards.

Its countywide political infrastructure intact, the Republican machine could rely on its networks in the construction and real estate industries and in credit and financing to actuate effective "racial steering" throughout the suburbs. The compliance of builders and realtors was assured primarily by the vertical integration of political appointments to the county administration, from supervisors to heads of agencies in charge of issuing building permits, licensure, and taxation. Information about suburban homes for sale, new developments under construction, sale prices, and financing opportunities were "tailored" according to the race of the prospective buyer. Pennsylvania laws overseeing construction lending and home financing favored local oversight and enabled discriminatory practices to occur with impunity. Out of state banks were restricted from lending in Pennsylvania, and in state banks were limited to lending in their home counties. According to McLarnon, in 1960 Delaware County was home to two large commercial banks, seven savings and loans, and twenty-five building and loan associations. The small size of the local banking community enhanced the machine's capacity to approve or deny suburban home mortgages on the basis of race. Although national in scope, the mortgage guarantee and home loan programs of the FHA and the Veterans Administration were not immune from the prevailing racial biases in the local housing market. Loan officers at Delaware Valley banks and savings and loans could easily apply subjective criteria to determine which applicants were qualified, had sufficient credit, and demonstrated the ability to pay for the homes they hoped to purchase.

McClure's Chester-based political organization did not cause suburbanization, nor was it responsible for the mass exodus of whites from Chester in the 1960s. But it clearly and effectively harnessed the racial fears among white city dwellers. Racial factors exerted far greater influence over the process of suburbanization than social class. While white flight is typically referenced in support of this claim, it is important to note that Chester's racial politics formed the basis for exclusion in the suburbs. The political machine that enveloped the suburbs and overlaid the patterns of racial segregation countywide had cut its teeth in Chester. The factors that accounted for whites leaving the city are less rooted in individualized racial prejudice and attitudes than in the institutional practices that harnessed racial fears into collective anxieties and an impulse to move. The stoking of racial fears in the city to underscore the "message" of racial integration and the threat of depressed property values that accompanied the encroachment of black residents into all-white, working-class neighborhoods rendered the exodus to the suburbs practical and beneficial to builders, realtors, banks, and politicians.

Toeing the Line in the Suburbs

The rise of Chester's suburbs was a spatial fix to the purportedly looming threat to whites of residential racial integration, stoked by institutional practices that both worsened the prospects for whites who remained in the city and offered sanctuary in the form of a single-family suburban home for those who left. By the late 1950s the underlying ethos of mass suburbanization was the idea that integration would damage white interests. For whites, relocating to the suburbs meant leaving behind city living and with it the prospect of living with black neighbors. The Republican machine's political incorporation of the suburbs promoted this spatial thinking of race relations and promised to enforce it. The degree of violent response to any breach of this "racial contract" demonstrates the commitment to the expanded racial divide in the era of mass suburbanization.

Together, the set of discriminatory suburban housing practices drummed up and reproduced on an everyday basis by real estate agents, loan officers, and builders proved a daunting obstacle to blacks seeking to own or rent homes, regardless of their social class status. The Republican War Board openly sanctioned the exclusionary practices of realtors and lenders and turned a blind eye to the intimidation and harassment of potential black buyers by home owner associations. The prevailing public discourse that normalized racial exclusion legitimized suburban exclusion. Ideology, public policy, and the actions of private actors locked up the postwar suburb as the privileged domain of whites. Individual and organized efforts to fight suburban racial exclusion were further challenged by a lack of recourse to state and federal fair housing laws. The Fair Housing Act, Title VIII of the Civil Rights Act, was not signed into law until 1968. Nonetheless, some blacks (along with white supporters) resisted the suburb's apparent racial order.

Quakers had long played a significant and active role in social justice issues in southeastern Pennsylvania, dating well before their principal roles in the Underground Railroad and the abolition movement. At the height of postwar suburbanization, Quakers prominently fought racial discrimination in residential real estate practices in Delaware County. In 1956 the early civil rights activist and realtor Margaret Collins founded Friends Suburban Housing Inc., a nondiscriminatory real estate brokerage firm. In the face of fierce opposition Collins pioneered efforts to sell homes in suburban Delaware County without regard to color. Meanwhile, other local fair housing advocates formed the Southeast Delaware County Area Committee of Friends Suburban Housing to lobby state and federal officials to pass antidiscriminatory legislation. These individuals spoke out against discrimination, often in conflict with fellow suburban Quakers who were concerned about their role in undoing stable communities. Broader support for integration among Quakers was not approved until May 1961, prompted by a statement printed in the *Swarthmorean*, the weekly paper of one of the county's more high toned suburban towns: "As individuals concerned with the community of Swarthmore, our country, and our world, we declare our conviction that neither the color of a man's skin, his nationality, nor his professed creed, are in any way related to his basic worth as an individual. We therefore believe that these characteristics should in no way prejudice the community's response to individuals who desire to enter our boundaries, visit our residents, work in our homes or businesses, eat, play, or live among us."[44] Collins and her associates networked with area black civic organizations to assist families interested in purchasing a home, pressured other realtors to provide inventories of homes for sale, and whenever possible, listed homes for sale by supportive sellers. Many of Collins's listings were homes foreclosed by the Veterans Administration. Friends Suburban Housing counseled black families before and after their moves to the suburbs and tempered the anger of white residents upset by the prospect of black neighbors.[45]

George Raymond, president of the Chester Branch of the NAACP, was one of the early clients of Friends Suburban Housing. A native of Chester, Raymond decided to relocate his family outside the city in the late 1950s. No stranger to the complications of fair housing and racial integration in Chester, he was acutely aware of the difficulties and potential dangers facing blacks moving to the suburbs. In the spring of 1958 the forty-four-year-old Raymond purchased an eight-room wooden frame farmhouse at 236 Sylvan Avenue in suburban Rutledge for $11,500. The Raymonds were the first black family to relocate to Rutledge, a small,

all-white suburb five miles northeast of Chester. Raymond purchased the house from the Veterans Administration, which took possession after the former owner defaulted on mortgage payments. Friends Suburban Housing held the property listing.

On May 24, one day prior to the family's planned move to their new home, an early morning fire consumed most of the house, rendering it uninhabitable. Although arson was immediately suspected, local fire officials cited the old electrical wiring as the likely cause. Two days before the fire, Raymond had requested the protection of the state attorney general's office, citing concerns for his family's safety based on a tip. A *Chester Times* reporter's interviews with the town's residents noted concerns that a black resident would spark an exodus of whites and a general resistance to "blacks mixing with whites" and "them living near me."

A number of Rutledge residents faulted the methods of Friends Suburban Housing, calling their efforts to racially integrate the town "aggressive and sneaky." Still others spoke of no communitywide prejudice but noted that black families should consider whether they would "fit into" Rutledge. As part of its effort to prevent violence and temper the hostility from townspeople, Friends Suburban Housing had already reached out to Raymond's future neighbors before the scheduled move in date. The realty firm found no organized or neighborhoodwide plan to resist or protest the Raymonds' intended move to Rutledge. Immediately after the fire, Raymond indicated that he and his family intended to rebuild the home. In February 1959, however, the Rutledge Borough Council passed an ordinance to condemn Raymond's home and take possession of the property. Citing eminent domain, the council planned to raze the home and build a previously undiscussed municipal building. A judge upheld Raymond's petition for an injunction after the town could not show adequate cause for taking possession of the property. A month later the council repealed the ordinance. Raymond had the home rebuilt, and he and his family moved to Rutledge.[46]

Subsequent attempts at suburban racial integration by Friends Suburban Housing met with both success and failure, if relatively unno-

Horace Baker (center, in checkered shirt) and his wife, Sarah (second from left), pause at the door of their new home in an all-white neighborhood in Folcroft, trailed by a crowd.

ticed. Unnoticed, that is, until the late summer of 1963, when Friends Suburban helped a young black family purchase a home in Folcroft, a Delaware County suburban bedroom community sandwiched between Philadelphia and Chester. The family's effort to move into their home set off what the local county newspaper called "a racial binge"—several nights of violence directed against the new home owners. The level of collective fury unleashed against a black couple and their young daughter in Folcroft was alarming; the incident revealed the intense commitment of whites to the suburbs as the spatial "corrective" to racial integration in the city.

In 1950, 1,900 people resided in Folcroft. By 1960 that number had risen to 7,861 residents, 3 of whom were black. Folcroft's Delmar Village of twelve hundred units, one of a number of modest suburban communities built in the 1950s, featured small, brick row houses with tidy, postage-stamp front yards. Its residents—all white—were a mix of skilled industrial workers and white-collar clerical workers, many of whom had moved to Folcroft from Philadelphia. In August 1963 Horace Baker and Sara Baker purchased a two-story brick row house with blue shutters for just over $11,000 through the Veterans Administration.

On the night Delmar Village residents learned that a black family had purchased the home, racial epithets were painted on its brick walls. In the two days that followed, all the house's windows were broken, its front and rear doors were severely damaged, and the plumbing and electrical systems were vandalized. A crowd varying in size from twenty to close to a thousand kept vigil in front of the home the day of the Bakers' anticipated arrival. The Bakers attempted to enter their home three times that day, only to be turned back by the angry mob. "A cursing, rock-throwing crowd estimated at five hundred persons threw yellow paint at their car and forced them to leave," described one account. "The men of Delmar Village, at least most of them, were at their jobs. Wives and children met the Bakers to protect the all-white community."[47] When the crowd reached close to a thousand, the Folcroft police chief requested the assistance of the state police, who quickly sealed off the neighborhood to keep the crowd from expanding. The next day the Bakers attempted to enter their home with an escort of state police patrol cars. Glenn A. McCurdy's 1964 account of the incident published in the *Negro Digest* describes the atmosphere prior to the Bakers' arrival: "Numbering about eight hundred as the arrival time approached, the gathering had the appearance of a harmless community outing, a family entertainment. Children played in the street, running among the legs of adults standing there; teenage boys sat on the hoods of police cars, legs dangling; and wives with their hair in curlers pushed baby carriages up closer to the center of festive excitement so they wouldn't miss anything."[48] McCurdy also recounts the intense jeering, swearing, and egg pelting directed at students from Chester's Crozer Theological Seminary and black and white ministers from local parishes who came to welcome the Bakers. After the Bakers arrived and entered their home, the mob swelled in size

Angry young boys gather at the Baker home, August 30, 1963.

and directed its animus at the state troopers ringing the home. The rock and bottle throwing continued into the night, subsiding around midnight. The Bakers' front lawn, according to McCurdy, was covered "an inch deep in broken glass and garbage."[49] Eventually, one hundred state troopers controlled the crowd outside the Bakers' home.[50]

One of the Bakers' failed attempts to move into their new home. August 29, 1963.

The day after the Bakers took possession of their home, one hundred Delmar Village home owners issued a statement to the media deploring the violence and blaming "outsiders" (the NAACP, among others). They called for a boycott of any business "which serves or deals with the Bakers." Their manifesto concluded: "We do not welcome the Baker family into our community. Perhaps this small borough can show this great nation that the federal government cannot force social integration upon the population."[51] In the weeks that followed, sporadic protests continued, but the violence and property damage subsided. Local ministers raised over $1,500 to help pay for repairs to the Bakers' home, and the local AFL-CIO (American Federation of Labor and Congress of Industrial Organizations) fronted the costs of labor for the repairs.[52] However, conditions did not improve and the Bakers endured verbal assaults and occasional violence to their home for months. In January 1964 the state Human Relations Commission filed injunction petitions against fifteen Delmar Village residents, including some borough officials, charging them with harassment. The state senate Democratic minority leader claimed that Folcroft was "synonymous with racial injustice throughout the world" and charged county and state officials with blatant indifference.[53] With the harassment unending, the Bakers sold their house in 1966.[54]

Given the scale of the protest and the extent of the mob violence, the "Folcroft incident" received considerable coverage in both the local and national media. But neither Rutledge nor Folcroft was unique; both resembled similar efforts to exclude blacks in postwar suburbs across the United States. Neighborhood home owner associations monitored home sales, recommended and worked with like-minded realtors, and organized petition drives aimed at black buyers with purchases in escrow or against leasing homes to blacks. Suburban racial exclusion was practiced institutionally by banks and realtors and individually by white home owners, reflecting the commonly held sentiment that blacks should not live in white neighborhoods. Accordingly, should blacks pose a threat, it stands to reason that exclusion was deemed rational at any cost.[55] Such thinking was prevalent in the working-class, first-ring suburbs that were home to large numbers of whites fleeing Chester and Philadelphia. More importantly, white county political leaders, home builders, lenders, and realtors legitimized racial exclusion explicitly or through unspoken actions. In addition to waging a difficult fight against housing discrimination, the work of Friends Suburban Housing laid bare the extent to which culpability was shared among the most vocal opponents to integration and those who remained silent.

On the whole, the political incorporation of the suburbs, the institutionalized mechanisms of racial exclusion, and the community-sanctioned intimidation and threats of violence prevailed, (re)producing the racial divide between Chester and the rest of Delaware County. Whites clearly dominated first-ring suburban towns surrounding Chester. The respective population numbers bear this out. Nearby Marcus Hook had 3,224 whites and 74 blacks; Tinicum 4,373 whites and 2 blacks; Eddystone 3,006 whites and 0 blacks.[56] Meanwhile, in Chester the 1960 census registered a population of 63,000, of which blacks numbered 27,000, just shy of half the city's residential total. Chester's total population declined by 2,300 (-3.5%) between 1950 and 1960, with the white population decreasing by 9,700 (-19.0%) and the black population increasing by 7,400 (53.0%). The full brunt of racial division was also becoming apparent. Chester's black unemployment rate in 1964 was 14 percent, compared to 7 percent for whites. In Delaware County the unemployment rate was 3.8 percent. Unemployment rates for blacks were twice as high as they were for whites in both 1950 and 1960. Most of the whites who left in the 1950s had higher education levels than the city average and were young adults and families leaving behind elderly parents (with lower education levels). The median age of the white population in 1960 was 32.3 years; for the black population, it was 18.7 years.[57]

Fear and the Intentionality of Exclusion

Chester's postwar suburbanization and the ensuing black and white divide between the city and the county were similar to the processes in other metropolitan regions in the Northeast and the Midwest after World War II. The suburbs offered the promise of comfort, open space, and newly built homes within commuting distance to factories and offices. Indeed, many city dwellers weary of noisy streets and older, tiny homes aspired to the suburban lifestyle. But the postwar suburb was for whites only, and our existing understandings of the important processes of racial steering, blockbusting, outright discrimination, violence, and communitywide prejudice clearly apply to Chester. This chapter has sought to highlight the significance of urban segregation to city-suburban racial division, especially the degree of political and administrative coordination involved in pushing the scale of racial exclusion to the regional level. Perhaps most importantly, this chapter underscored the intentionality, not the inevitability, of suburban exclusion, that suburban development was a collective spatial fix that fed on and amplified white fear of and uncertainty about racial integration. The ideology of racial division was the guiding strategy of the stakeholders in the spatial development of the suburbs. Consequently, Chester was increasingly hamstrung politically and economically, as outlined in the next chapter. The resulting turmoil of the 1960s civil rights era proved to be yet another instance of race used as a strategy to promote spatial change.

4

The Birmingham of the North

Notwithstanding the considerable economic and social changes cities faced after World War II, in many ways black-white divisions in Chester remained simply more of the same. The departure of whites to working-class suburbs immediately to the north and west of the city continued apace. The stream of southern black families moving north for employment slowed somewhat as older manufacturing firms relocated or downsized, but in combination with new families, the city's black population continued its steady rise. Yet in everyday terms the shrinking of Chester's white population and the rise in black residents changed little in the racial status quo that governed core aspects of everyday life—where people lived, worked, went to school, bought groceries and clothes, saw movies, and ate meals. Chester's boomtown feel still resonated in the early 1950s regardless of steady but small yearly declines in its manufacturing output since the end of the war effort. Downtown Chester was the center for shopping in the expanding Delaware County, with Sears and Roebuck and Kresge's 5 and 10 dominating a vibrant business district populated by restaurants, beauty salons, barbershops, shoe stores, corner stores, banks, bowling alleys, and movie theaters. And whereas black residents were welcome to spend their money downtown, most businesses hired few black workers, and many maintained separate facilities for their black customers well into the late 1950s.

Postwar demographic and economic changes slowly put pressure on the city's long-standing racial status quo and the seeming permanence of white-privileged Chester. Federal court rulings and national legislation targeting the segregation of schools and housing magnified the "work" of Chester's white elites and institutions to maintain homegrown racial inequality. In hindsight and given the depth of commit-

Speare Brothers Department Store, 7th Street and Edgemont Street, 1961, founded in 1921 and closed in 1973. Reproduced by permission of the Delaware County Historical Society, Pa.

ment to segregation, the civil rights movement's disruption of the racial status quo seemed inevitable. As this chapter recounts, Chester's civil rights struggle in the early 1960s also factored into the local politics of suburbanization.

Chester's established civil rights leaders won incremental gains in improving conditions for black residents in the 1950s. The challenge to the racial status quo took a spectacular and explosive turn in the early 1960s. Over the course of five years Chester emerged as one of the key battlegrounds in the nation's civil rights movement, earning the city a national reputation for public racial unrest. In the spring of 1964 the national director of the Congress of Racial Equality (CORE) called Chester "the Birmingham of the North."[1]

Civil rights activism has deep roots in Chester, as local religious lead-ers and the NAACP advanced the cause of racial integration during the peak of overt racial antagonism and institutional discrimination in the 1940s and 1950s. This chapter provides an overview of early leaders and efforts before turning to a discussion of complex cleavages and oppos-ing agendas in the black and white communities set on challenging or preserving the city's racial status quo. As was the case nationally, internal struggles over tactics and the pace of change divided Chester's main civil rights organization in the early 1960s. Beyond describing the internal dynamics of civil rights activism, however, this chapter shows how local political leaders shaped and manipulated organized mass dissent against racial segregation and discrimination to benefit their own political aims and financial objectives, namely, furthering the racial divide between the city and the suburbs. In addition to feeding divisions within the black activist community, white elites benefited in a self-serving way from fan-ning the white fears of racial violence and unrest that they deceptively sanctioned. Chester's civil rights activism, then, unfolded against a back-drop of elite, seemingly contradictory interests in protecting the racial status quo and white privilege while exacerbating whites' fears of civil unrest that fed an exodus to the suburbs.

Chester's ruling white Republican machine had already eased the mi-gration of fellow whites from the city to the suburbs, politically coloniz-ing newly formed towns and unincorporated suburbs and extending its system of political favors to sway suburban residential and commercial developers, bankers, investors, and other business elites—all of whom benefited handsomely from the white exodus from Chester that trebled after the racial unrest and violence of the summer of 1964. They capital-ized on visceral racial antagonism and fear, the unsustainability of the racial status quo in the city itself, and the failed efforts by local whites to hunker down and maintain privileges to the exclusion of Chester's black residents. In the 1960s the Republican machine, now fully invested in the city-suburban racial divide, allowed the racial status quo it had helped build and orchestrate in Chester to fully unravel.

This story of racial manipulation suggests that the processes that led to the condition of the impacted ghetto, a story often explained as the result of large-scale economic and labor market changes in the American economy, have their foundations in a political agency that favored the exodus of white people and capital over racial compromise and integration. As this chapter demonstrates, white elites intentionally interceded in Chester's civil rights campaign by covertly ratcheting up the scale of protests, answering them publicly with violent "law and order" crackdowns, and squashing efforts at compromise that might lead to racial integration. This duplicitous political strategy heightened racial antagonisms among residents in the city itself, ultimately ushering in black political control (described in later chapters) of a city economically and socially hamstrung by the flight of white residents and white-owned small businesses (and their capital).

Economic and Demographic Challenges to the Racial Divide

In many ways Chester's economic and demographic changes a decade after the end of World War II duplicated those of small northeastern manufacturing cities such as nearby Camden, New Jersey, and Wilmington, Delaware, and larger ones such as Baltimore and Philadelphia. The waterfront industries continued to be the main sources of employment throughout the 1950s and 1960s, although the number of manufacturing firms and positions steadily declined over time. Sun Shipbuilding, Scott Paper, and the Philadelphia Electric Company remained the city's biggest employers. Baldwin Locomotive closed. The Ford assembly plant shut down in 1960, shedding 2,300 manufacturing jobs. Total manufacturing employment in Delaware County declined 12 percent from 1950 to 1962, and between 1958 and 1962 the number of county manufacturing establishments fell from 415 to 385. Unemployment was 9.3 percent in Chester compared to 3.0 percent for the entire county. Black unemployment in the city was 14.2 percent, double that of whites at 7.2 percent.[2]

In comparison with suburban Delaware County, Chester's labor force was concentrated in industrial manufacturing and low-paying service positions. In 1960 only 9 percent of Chester workers were employed in white collar clerical, professional, and managerial positions, compared to 17 percent for Delaware County. The median family income in Chester of $5,343 was considerably less than the county's $7,289, reflecting the migration of middle- and high-income families out of the city into the suburbs. Indicative of residential suburbanization, Chester "imported" 11,500 employees from the rest of Delaware County while exporting 6,600 workers to jobs in the rest of the county. The out-migration of mostly whites occurred in tandem with the in-migration of blacks, whose prospects and earnings in manufacturing and service positions were curtailed. The 1959 median income for Chester's black families was $4,059, less than 70 percent of the $5,880 median income for white families. A third of Chester's families lived in poverty, with black families comprising 50 percent of the city's poor and whites 25 percent.[3]

Chester's economic changes were coupled with dramatic shifts in its population, especially in relation to the expanding suburbs of Delaware County. In 1950 Chester's population comprised 16 percent of Delaware County; in 1960 the city's total population of 63,700 comprised 11 percent of the county. As cited earlier, the total population had declined by 2,300 (-3.5%) between 1950 and 1960, with the white population decreasing by 9,700 (-19%) and the black population increasing by 7,400 to 27,000 (53%). Most of the whites who left for the suburbs in the 1950s were young, newly formed families with higher education levels than the city average. Overall, the city's population in 1960 was a shrinking community of older, working-class whites (with a median age of 32.3 years) and a growing number of young blacks (with a median age of 18.7 years).[4] Black residents over the age of 25 averaged 8.4 years of schooling. Residential segregation prevailed, with over 80 percent of the entire black population residing in five contiguous census tracts in the central part of the city.[5]

Old Guard Civil Rights Challenges to the Racial Divide

Unsurprisingly, Chester's decades-old racial status quo creaked and groaned under the weight of the vast changes in the city's economy and the composition of its population. The city's black civil rights activists viewed the changes as an opportunity for racial progress but not as an occasion to shift their tried-and-true tactics of quiet resistance. Chester's Old Guard civil rights activists kept to a pragmatic gradualist approach that relied on a mix of compromise with political elites and court challenges to compel white institutions to change. In the struggle to integrate schools, many older black residents were reminded that leaders working on behalf of white political elites provided important results, such as the opening of all-black schools and the hiring of black teachers and administrators in the 1930s. Thirty years later McClure appointees still served on the school board and hired principals and teachers who were "faithful" to the city-county patronage machine. They served as ward leaders and liaisons between the black community and white elites but functioned primarily as eyes and ears on the ground reporting directly to the political machine. Civil rights activists were consistently reminded that working with the local politics of the racial status quo defined (and defended) by whites was the prudent path to change, however slow and piecemeal. Local civil rights activists, ministers, and community organizers worked through the NAACP, choosing their battles with the white establishment and compromising, albeit reluctantly, to achieve results. They were older and had spent decades at work slowly carving out modest advantages for the city's black community amid considerable racial hostility. By the early 1960s they found their brand of political action challenged by a new climate of assertive activism, both nationally and locally.

For two decades Barbour, pastor of Calvary Baptist Church, was the chief strategist of local civil rights activism. His reputation as a black leader was defined by his ability to work across racial lines to improve the everyday conditions of Chester's blacks. An intellectual as well as

NOTICE !

STOP LOOK AND READ

THE N. A. A. C. P.

wishes to report to the public business places who previously refused Negro patronage but now

HAVE CHANGED THEIR POLICY !

YOU CAN NOW BE SERVED

IN THE FOLLOWING PLACES

1. The Highway Diner, 9th & Lamokin St.
2. Shooster's Curb Service, 9th & Flower St.
3. Crystal Restaurant, 4th & Edgmont Ave.
4. Goff's, 8th & Edgmont Ave.
5. Circle, 3rd & Market St.

YOU CAN ALSO SIT ANYWHERE

IN THE FOLLOWING THEATRES

1. Strand Theatre, 3rd & Reaney
2. Apollo, 3rd & Lloyd
3. Washington, 4th & Market
4. Stanley, Fourth and Edgmont
5. State, 7th and Edgmont

If anyone is discriminated by any of the said business places or know of any business practicing discrimination please notify at once

George Raymond

1704 READING DRIVE   PHONE 2-6237

Watch for N.A.A.C.P. Bulletins for our next Mass Meeting.

NAACP Bulletin, 1948. Courtesy of the George Raymond Papers, Widener University Archives.

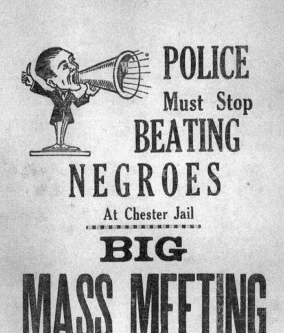

Calvary Baptist Church Meeting Flyer, 1952. Courtesy of the George Raymond Papers, Widener University Archives.

a spiritual leader, Barbour's measured and pragmatic approach to civil rights activism earned the respect of Chester's blacks and white elites and drew national attention. In Chester Barbour was change advocate and peacemaker.

> When pastoral duties were done for the day, one might see Rev. Barbour strolling along West Third Street, his black derby sitting at a rakish angle, sporting horn-rimmed spectacles and dangling a giant cigar between his teeth. At times he paused to chat with young folks or stood in front of the pool hall along with some of its habitués. Very often he would visit the office of Alderman Casper H. Green where local political figures frequently held court in the smoke-filled back-room. . . . Pius never failed to pen off letters to newspapers expressing himself on various issues. . . . Seldom getting actively involved in civic or political controversies, Barbour nevertheless maintained a friendly balance between the "Old Guard" and the "New Negro" as the leaders of the two Black factions were beginning to be characterized.[6]

Barbour played the diplomat to Raymond's predilection to threaten legal action to advance the civil rights agenda. But Raymond too was a pragmatist. In his early years as president of the local NAACP, he had worked to end the segregation of public accommodations in restaurants, theaters, and hotels. That experience led him to believe that Chester was a closed society and that the only way to bring about change was to acknowledge and work with the entrenched Republican political machine that governed the city and had successfully co-opted the elites of the black community. Working with Barbour, Raymond understood that piecemeal reforms could accumulate as real progress over time.[7]

Both Barbour and Raymond viewed the odds of upending Chester's legacy of racial segregation as shifting in their favor. Thanks to suburbanization, Chester was fast becoming a majority black city. The national civil rights movement was making progress even in the Deep South. Economic and demographic changes threatened to upset Chester's racial order, as the boundaries of white neighborhoods slowly gave way in the wake of continued white flight and expanding numbers of black residents in need of housing. The racial covenants and other collective, neighborhoodwide efforts to defend the status quo tore at the seams, as individual home owners chose the expediency (and money) of renting or selling to black families over a commitment to racial order. Chester's decades-old racial status quo was clearly not sustainable.

Challenging public school segregation proved much more difficult, however. For decades the local chapter of the NAACP, with support from black churches, kept the demand to end segregated public education at the top of the local civil rights agenda but achieved little success. White parent associations compelled the school board to aggressively defend racially segregated schools. In 1946 the NAACP worked with a committee of black parents to organize a student strike at a decrepit and overcrowded elementary school, demanding integration of students and teachers (who were assigned to work at black or white schools according to their race). In the fall of 1946 the school board agreed to integrate the city's public schools. But the decision held only symbolic value, as organized opposition by white parents delayed changes and an administrative loophole permitted them to transfer their children to predominantly white schools.

In the fifteen years following the school board's promise to end segregation, very little changed in Chester's public education. In 1954 Raymond threatened to take additional legal actions after the U.S. Supreme Court in *Brown v. Board of Education of Topeka* declared separate public schools for black and white students unconstitutional. In response to the *Brown* decision and ensuing threats of lawsuits, the Chester school board devised and implemented a "neighborhood schools" plan to legally comply with the desegregation of Chester public schools. Neighborhood schools would accept all students regardless of race, creed, or color, based on their residence within neighborhoods whose boundaries were determined by the board. Chester's school board, elected politicians, and white residents found this decision palatable and easy to accomplish, especially given that residential segregation would ensure the de facto racial segregation of schools.

The board's policy of neighborhood schools, in effect, hardened its commitment to segregation. As the racial composition of the city changed, the neighborhood schools policy remained intact save for the redrawing of neighborhood boundaries to reflect the shrinking sizes of white neighborhoods. The board first established neighborhood boundary lines in August 1954 that reflected the racial topography of Chester. An investigation in 1964 revealed evidence of unofficial redrawing, including an enlargement of the zone for the all-black schools to reflect the growth of a black neighborhood. Consequently, public education in Chester in the early 1960s resembled that of fifteen years earlier: one high school, four junior high schools, and eleven elementary schools. With the exception of the racially integrated high school, all the other schools were either fully or highly segregated. In 1963 the enrollment in three of the eleven elementary schools was 100 percent black, while two others were just over 80 percent. The black majority schools were "mostly old wooden structures, poorly heated, crumbling plaster walls and ceilings, with peeling paint, drafty windows, small classrooms, and inadequate bathroom facilities, with 'hand-me-down' books provided to black schoolchildren." The number of black teachers comprised just under a third of the four hundred and fifty teachers employed by the Chester school system.[8] With aging infrastructure, poor funding, and overcrowding, school standards and performance continued to decline, as exemplified in the case of Franklin Elementary School. Built in 1910 for an enrollment of five hundred students, the school was never remodeled or expanded. In 1963 the school's enrollment stood at just over one thousand students, 99 percent of whom were black.[9]

Local church and civil rights leaders challenged the Chester School Board's neighborhood school policy on the grounds that it fostered the segregation of students and educators. The board acknowledged that a racial imbalance existed in individual schools but contended that this was an outcome of prevailing residential patterns, not board actions or policies. As such, school board leaders claimed they were neither legally bound nor financially able to address or fix the root residential causes of racial imbalance. "We have no segregation in the Chester schools. To talk about *de facto* segregation is not to talk about segregation but about a condition over which we have no control."[10] Regarding the demand that the district apportion all public schoolteachers to achieve the same proportion of black teachers to white teachers in each school, the board contended that teacher assignments were based on qualifications and educational reasons, not racial ones. In a moment of convenient historical amnesia, the board reminded the NAACP that Chester's black community leaders had successfully petitioned the board for black schools with black teachers and administrators in the 1920s, three decades prior to the ruling that racial segregation was unconstitutional. The special counsel for the school board summed up the district's position:

> Most people think that the Chester School Board are guilty of segregation, that we take school children and because they are black, we send them to Negro schools. Most people think that we take children and because they are white, we send them to white schools. That's what they think we are doing. . . . Now is the School Board responsible for the geography of the city of Chester? . . . But the geography of our city is a physical fact which has to be taken into consideration. Another physical fact is where the people live. The School Board has nothing to do with where people live. That's a result of our society and a lot of conditions that all of us are very sorry about and trying to help in our feeble way, but it's not something that's in the control of the Chester School Board. . . . So what we're talking about in Chester is not anything done by the School Board in the manner of segregation but the result of a social problem that has arisen over many, many years with very deplorable results, results that we all regret very, very much.[11]

The NAACP and the school board remained locked in protracted legal battles in which the board legally complied on paper while the NAACP sought to show institutional culpability in de facto school segregation. Both parties looked to the courts for a resolution. In the decade following the *Brown* decision, the school board maintained that it was up to the courts "to decide the question whether the maintenance and operation of a racially segregated public school system is lawful and non-discriminatory where such segregation allegedly arises out of racially segregated residential patterns in the City of Chester."[12] Meanwhile, the NAACP continued to rely on negotiation, compromise, and a legal course of action when necessary.

For its part, McClure's Republican political machine easily tolerated and perhaps even accommodated the gradual pace and civil tone of local civil rights activism. Raymond and Barbour were reformists; neither threatened the underlying political basis of the racial status quo or the machine's political and economic venture in the expanding suburbs. In the Annual Report of NAACP Branch Activities for 1961, for example, the local branch secretary reported to the national office: "There is something wrong with Chester. . . . The people here seem to live a carefree life. They seem to want us to fight their battles and don't want to help." The same report held the local Republican political machine accountable: "Chester is owned and operated by one man, Mr. John McClure. The people here seem afraid of this man's organization. . . . Mr. John McClure has Chester sewed up, the people here seem afraid of losing their jobs or other things."[13]

As the civil rights movement in the South and large cities in the North turned to tactics of civil disobedience and direct action, Chester's strategy of quiet persistence seemed antiquated and increasingly inadequate. By the early 1960s the national civil rights movement, far from abandoning legal efforts to end segregation, had nonetheless begun to favor other movement tactics, such as direct action and collective protest. Chester's young blacks in particular did not share Raymond's patience with working with the political machine and grew frustrated with the slow pace of change. Consequently, membership in the organization declined; membership in 1962 was less than half of that in 1958. Chester's black-white divide was no longer sustainable, but neither was the strategy of civil rights gradualism.

The question of de facto segregation in Chester was ultimately settled by commissions and courts but not before an upstart civil rights movement tried to end local racial discrimination through ongoing demonstrations in 1964, as outlined in the following section. As expected, politicians, the police, and the white and black ward lieutenants of the Republican machine denounced the civil unrest, sought to contain it, and eventually responded with state violence. But months of street demonstrations and protests revealed another side of the Republican machine's role: whites' fears of racial unrest were manipulated to further the demographic and spatial changes already enveloping the region. McClure's hand in the civil unrest of 1963 does not diminish the intentions and purposes of collective action against racial discrimination. Rather, it reveals how powerful stakeholders can use the racial divide to further their political and economic interests in urban change. The aftermath of the unrest revealed that the Republican machine had little to lose and much to gain by ending the city's racial status quo. The new realities of Chester and Delaware County—the exodus of the city's white residents, the growth in its black population, and the intentional shift of political and economic power to the suburbs—meant the status quo in Chester was not sustainable even for the established political order. The question facing political leaders was how to favorably influence the outcome of black dissent.

Civil Rights Activism and Urban Unrest

Chester's advocates for a more visible mass politics of collective civil rights action found a leader in Stanley Branche, a twenty-eight-year-old activist who came to Chester in 1962 and immediately began to shake up the local civil rights movement. Branche single-handedly brought the civil rights repertoire of pickets, sit-ins, and demonstrations to Chester. Within a few months Branche emerged as both hero and villain of

Chester's civil rights movement, but not necessarily along black and white lines. A report published after a year of racial protests and violence noted, "The Chester demonstrations and the whole present Chester civil rights movement have been essentially shaped by Stanley Branche."[14]

Upon his arrival in Chester, Branche worked in the organizational ranks of Raymond's NAACP. But he soon grew impatient with the slow pace of the organization. Branche criticized the antipopulist back room deals occasionally struck between NAACP leaders and white politicians and school board members. He lobbied the local NAACP to adopt direct action and mass protest tactics that would give the vast majority of Chester's black men and women a meaningful stake in the immediate improvement of civil rights. Branche's democratic tactics found little support among Old Guard gradualists, who worried that confrontation would upset order, prompt violence, and ultimately backfire. Undeterred and without permission, Branche began to recruit activists sympathetic to his call for direct action from inside the NAACP; Swarthmore, the nearby suburban liberal arts college; and the Swarthmore chapter of the Students for a Democratic Society (SDS) Economic Research and Action Project (ERAP). He formed the NAACP Young Adults to "put life into the Chester civil rights movement"[15] as a direct action unit within (but not controlled by) the local chapter, placing the organization in the awkward position of providing emergency assistance to its dissenting members.[16]

In an attempt to quell or perhaps manage the growing dissent instigated by Branche, Raymond suggested the compromise tactic of threatening direct action and protests to compel change among white institutions. In April 1963 Raymond worked with Branche to challenge the hiring practices of downtown Chester's large department stores, clothing shops, shoe stores, and other specialty shops. Although the shops welcomed (however reluctantly) increasing numbers of black residents as customers, the vast majority of retail employees were white. The two threatened the Chester Businessmen's Association with a protracted boycott and pickets by black customers unless shops committed to hiring black employees. The prospect of a boycott worked. The association soon adopted a policy ensuring fair employment practices.[17] But Branche was interested in more than the threat of civil disobedience.

Stoking Divisions within the Civil Rights Movement

In June 1963 Cecil Moore, the president of the Philadelphia NAACP, delivered a reproachful speech to a crowd of two hundred gathered at Bethany Baptist Church in Chester. Moore directly challenged Old Guard gradualism on Raymond's turf, urging, "Negroes of Chester should not be afraid to burn shoe leather in picket lines and should not be afraid to go to jail fighting for their rights." He reprimanded Chester's black working and middle classes, including prominent ministers, attorneys, doctors, and politicians, for their blind commitment to "Uncle Tomism." He took aim at the Republican Party machine, calling parts of the city "McClure's pasture," where a black man "sells his soul, gives up his rights for the privilege of participating in numbers, prostitution, gambling or for getting a ticket fixed or holding a political job for which he is not qualified."[18] Moore's passionate speech may not have disclosed anything new, but it publicly acknowledged the cleavages between the Old Guard and the "New Negro" in Chester's civil rights movement, lending legitimacy to the demands of younger activists led by Branche.

The well-worn conventional strategies for bringing about progressive change in Chester were quickly challenged. Chester's mayor, Joseph L. Eyre, formed the Chester Human Relations Commission and turned to Raymond to recommend individuals to serve on its board. The NAACP Young Adults protested, charging that some of Raymond's choices were "politically bound" with connections to the Republican machine, and that his seniority "doesn't mean he represents the entire Negro community."[19] The internal dispute over legitimate appointees was never resolved, relegating the commission to the sidelines of the civil rights movement. Raymond felt obligated to remind the public that "general NAACP policy or expressions of official NAACP views on current prob-

lems will continue to come from me, as president, or from someone specifically designated to speak for me." The *Delaware County Daily Times*
capitalized on the apparent rift within the organization, editorializing
that "some feel he [Branche] is a headline grabber using the civil rights
issue to boost himself."[20]

In the fall of 1963 Branche formally resigned from the NAACP, taking
several younger members with him and forming a new activist organization, the Committee for Freedom Now (CFFN).[21] His resignation,
however, did not signal a final break with the NAACP, whose response
to Branche and the CFFN was evasive. The national office officially dis-
approved of Branche's flagrant disregard of organizational policies and
local authority and branded him a rogue troublemaker and media dem-
agogue. Yet in contrast with Raymond's old guard activism, Branche's
firebrand style promised to reinvigorate Chester's civil rights struggle.
The NAACP feared becoming irrelevant as younger blacks across the
United States demanded quicker social change. Regarding Chester, the
national office blamed Raymond for improperly handling Branche and
not keeping him in the fold of the local chapter. The deputy executive
director of the NAACP noted, "Methinks Raymond created a Franken-
stein in Branche, let him get out of hand, failed himself to provide aggressive leadership."

In the remaining months of 1963, the national office pursued two
seemingly contradictory solutions to the Branche-Raymond "Chester
problem": to co-opt Branche and bring him and the CFFN back into
the fold and to distance itself from Branche by pointing out that the
CFFN's tactics were incompatible with the civil rights cause. In either
case, Raymond appeared left out. With the tacit approval of the national
office and unbeknownst to Raymond, the NAACP's regional secretary
had supported Branche in organizing the Chester branch's younger
members and forming the CFFN. Upon learning of the NAACP's role,
Raymond protested, "We have an NAACP field secretary forming a new
group, further dividing the small army of responsible citizens and the
money available—evidently supported by the NAACP." The national of-

fice responded that Branche "has no official capacity at the present time with the NAACP."[22]

Branche's CFFN took on Raymond's long-term cause: an immediate end to overcrowding and poor conditions at black schools and the larger goal of public school integration. In November 1963 CFFN protesters blocked the entrance of Franklin Elementary and followed with additional protests at the Chester Municipal Building; 240 protesters were arrested. Public attention, stoked by media coverage of the mass arrests, forced the mayor and the school board, in a meeting with Branche and Phillip Savage, the NAACP's regional director, to agree to make physical improvements at the school and transfer 165 of its students to reduce overcrowding. Encouraged by the successful outcome of Chester's first mass demonstration, the CFFN took full credit. Branche told the local media "that the Board of Education had given in to many of CFFN's demands."[23] In light of the successful school protest, Raymond reluctantly invited Branche and Savage to a Chester NAACP branch meeting. Neither man showed up. Instead, a small group of CFFN members still affiliated with the NAACP's youth organization arrived carrying placards protesting the NAACP's feeble support of Chester's awakened civil rights movement. At the meeting one protester asked Raymond if he was tied to Chester's Republican Party machine.

The CFFN successfully seized control of the school issue, sponsoring boycotts and organizing mass demonstrations against Chester's segregated schools in the first half of 1964. Mayor Eyre was replaced by James H. Gorbey, who publicly condemned the boycotts and demonstrations and instituted a policy of arresting persons "blocking traffic and entrances to buildings in the course of demonstrations."[24] The stakes became higher in March when the Chester Human Relations Commission formally recommended integration of the elementary school faculties by the next school term and development of a plan for integration of the student bodies. The school board immediately rejected the commission's recommendation, sticking to its claim that there was nothing it could do about the racial imbalance in the schools caused by the segregation of the city's neighborhoods.[25] Facing public uproar over the board's refusal to change its policies, Raymond again reached out to Branche to join forces.

Just as the NAACP signed on to the CFFN's agenda of protesting de facto segregation in public schools, Branche upped the ante by inviting the controversial activist Malcolm X to speak in Chester. On March 11, 1964 Raymond sent a handwritten note to the NAACP deputy executive director reporting on his progress with Branche: "I believe he's coming back into the fold—some of his group will meet with the Chester NAACP Board tomorrow night." In a postscript he added, "Provided he cancels Malcolm X." On March 14 Malcolm X, speaking in Chester, obliquely referenced the CFFN-NAACP split:

> We should be peaceful, law-abiding, but the time has come for the American Negro to fight back in self-defense whenever and where ever he is being unjustly and unlawfully attacked. . . . The political philosophy of Black Nationalism means: We must control the politics and the politicians of our community. They must no longer take orders from outside forces. We will organize and sweep out of office all Negro politicians who are puppets for the outside forces. Whites can help us, but they can't join us. There can be no black-white unity until there is first some black unity.[26]

Raymond immediately issued a statement distancing the NAACP from Malcolm X's visit, Branche, and the CFFN: "The Chester NAACP does not endorse Malcolm X nor those groups and individuals who tacitly or openly support him."[27] Raymond was quoted in the local press as saying, "Malcolm X's statements regarding violence are not only incompatible with the program of the NAACP but are designed to create an aura of suspicion and misapprehension among white persons regarding peaceful and lawful demonstrations sponsored by legitimate and established civil rights groups."[28]

A dozen church ministers telegrammed the national office in anger over the NAACP-CFFN alliance. In response, the NAACP promised to

Civil rights leaders Lawrence Landry (SNIC-Chicago), Gloria Richardson (Cambridge, Md.), Comedian Dick Gregory, Malcolm X (New York City), and Stanley Branche (Chester). March 14, 1964, Chester, Pa.

end its ties with Branche and the CFFN unless both "completely disavow their association with Malcolm X and the philosophy he represents."[29] At the same time, the national office continued to pressure the Chester branch to endorse and participate in CFFN-sponsored mass demonstrations or risk being left behind and becoming irrelevant to the next generation of activists. Branche's contact in the NAACP convinced him to issue a short declaration stating that Malcolm X's appearance at a "multi-sponsored meeting does not imply an endorsement of his principles."[30]

In the first half of 1964 Branche offered Chester a novel brand of civil rights activism that generated a great deal of press attention, deep controversy within the black community, and tensions between the local and the national NAACP leaderships. Branche routinely and provocatively railed against the school board, the police department, and the Republican political machine, generating headlines and undoing Raymond's legacy of quiet pressure and patient tenacity. In a city systematically governed for generations by institutions anchored in securing white privilege, Branche's radicalism appealed to many local blacks and shocked and angered whites and conservative blacks. For Branche's expanding numbers of supporters, months of mass demonstrations and protests meant risking life and limb to undo once and for all the city's legacy of deep-seated racism. For Raymond, Barbour, and other Old Guard activists, the risk of backlash from the political establishment was matched only by their ongoing suspicion and apprehension of the larger-than-life Branche.

Raising the Stakes of Civil Rights Activism in 1964

Emboldened by the Franklin Elementary School demonstrations, the CFFN recruited new members and began to plan its next moves. In January 1964 the organization opened a storefront recruitment center, sponsored a voter registration campaign, and prepared for a scheduled citywide boycott of Chester's public schools.[31] By spring the CFFN leadership and the Chester police were embroiled in a tit-for-tat struggle over demonstrator tactics and law enforcement response, each ratcheting up the stakes. Ultimately, the police violently cracked down on civil disobedience.

As CFFN leader, Branche planned and directly coordinated a combination of marches, sit-ins, boycotts, and mass demonstrations at targeted institutions (mainly schools and city hall) and commercial streets in the central business district. Throughout the spring unrest, Branche acted as press spokesperson, community liaison, recruiter, and chief negotiator. He nurtured ties with student groups at Pennsylvania Military College, Swarthmore College, and Cheyney State College to ensure large turnouts at marches and demonstrations.[32] With few exceptions, the direct action campaigns were large in numbers; frequent (eventually daily); and disruptive to business, government functions, and pedestrian and vehicular traffic.[33] On March 27, for example, three hundred protesters marched from a church rally in the West End to the downtown business district escorted by the entire Chester police force of seventy officers. Police arrested three protesters for impeding traffic, prompting all the remaining demonstrators to sit down at a busy shopping intersection. The protesters dispersed after Branche received a tip that sixty Pennsylvania state troopers had been called as backup.[34] On the next day the CFFN staged simultaneous midday sit-down demonstrations to intentionally shut down traffic in downtown Chester. Over two hundred protesters assembled in front of the CFFN office, where they were instructed to march together downtown, disperse into small groups, sit in key intersections, sing and clap, and "play dead" if confronted and arrested by the police. The multiple sit-down tactic worked. Downtown traffic came to a standstill, and dozens of white office workers, sales clerks, and curious shoppers lined the sidewalks to gawk at protesters. The police response was swift and violent. On March 28 the *Delaware County Daily Times* described the incident at Seventh and Edgemont Streets: "Club-swinging city police halted a racial sit-down at the busiest intersection in the city this afternoon." On March 30 the same paper said that on March 28 police had "moved in, swinging riot sticks." All the protesters were arrested.[35]

Protesters responded to the violent crackdown by the police with even larger demonstrations. Ordinary Chester citizens, outraged by the images of passive demonstrators beaten with nightsticks and dragged off to waiting buses, filled the streets to oppose the escalation of police violence. The atmosphere downtown became so tense that the anticipated nightly standoffs between police and protesters overshadowed the original objectives of the demonstrations. Branche took to the airwaves, calling for massive civil disobedience to the police response. The demonstrations grew larger, with an estimated three hundred and fifty persons marching into the center of the city and around the police station on April 2. That day Mayor Gorbey issued "The Police Position to Preserve the Public Peace," a ten-point statement promising an immediate return to "law and order."[36] The city deputized firemen and trash collectors to handle demonstrators. The mayor formally requested the assistance of the state police. April witnessed successive nights with hundreds of demonstrators arrested and dozens beaten. All Chester's public schools closed on April 22 amid fears for student safety. With no end in sight, Mayor Gorbey spoke to the slim chance of a negotiated truce: "There's only one man out there and that's Stanley Branche that could get them to declare a moratorium [on demonstrations]. And I don't believe that I could be the person to ask him."

Police retribution climaxed late in the evening of April 22, a night of brutality that a commission appointed by the governor later called "the straw that broke the camel's back." That evening Chester police and eighty Pennsylvania State Police troopers surprised a group of three hundred protesters who rallied at the police station. A small cadre of Chester police officers demanded that demonstrators stop singing and disperse or face arrest. Some protesters dispersed, but others began to march until the police physically blocked them. About forty Chester police officers and the state troopers "came in a group with a great rush out of the police station" to disperse the demonstrators.[37] Dozens were beaten. At a mass rally against police brutality two nights later, more violence ensued, as the state police again assisted in forcibly dispersing protesters. That night a large number of state police officers burst into the Bull Moose Bar at Third and Lamokin Streets around midnight and "surrounded, cursed, and indiscriminately beat the male and female occupants."[38] On the night of Saturday, April 25 there was "so much tension in Chester that one hardly dared light a match."[39] Only the governor's intervention on April 26 prevented a "grave race war."[40] Altogether, over six hundred people had been arrested during approximately two months of civil rights rallies, marches, pickets, boycotts, and sit-ins.[41]

Understanding the "Chester Situation"

The protests of 1964 energized the local struggle against entrenched racial segregation in Chester. The sheer number of local residents, the commitment to a costly and unrelenting campaign, and the consistent threat and frequent occurrence of intimidation and physical violence upended the old order that had defined the city's history for decades. Given the degree of the local white political establishment's commitment to racial inequality across employment, housing, education, and everyday activities, the civil rights movement in Chester was clearly an accomplishment, especially for the individual women, men, and children who vowed to bring about real change.

In the weeks following the April unrest, the CFFN collected dozens of statements from protesters who suffered or witnessed excessive use of force by police on April 22 and April 24 and presented them to the Human Relations Commission.[42] Although the commission was highly critical of civil rights leaders for calling for continuous demonstrations and considered the sit-ins illegal, it did find in favor of the protesters: "There is reason to believe that the political 'power structure' was unsympathetic with the immediacy of demands of the Negro community and that this attitude was to some extent reflected in the methods adopted by the police to repress the demonstrations."[43]

The Chester demonstrations also prompted the state to take action on long-standing racial problems. At a meeting in Philadelphia with the state attorney general, the mayor of Chester, the city solicitor, and representatives of the Pennsylvania Human Relations Commission, Governor William Scranton ordered public hearings on the charges of de facto segregation in Chester schools.[44] While the Pennsylvania Human Relations Commission held hearings during the summer of 1964, all protests and demonstrations ceased. In November the commission issued its final order requiring the desegregation of schools and an end to the practice of assigning only black teachers, stenographers, clerks, and bookkeepers to predominantly black schools. The commission found that although the Chester School Board was "aware or should have been aware of the existence of segregated schools within its system, it did not act at any time to attempt to correct this condition."[45] The school district appealed the ruling and the commonwealth court partially ruled in the district's favor, stating that the commission did not substantiate its charges of intentional segregation. The court did uphold the commission's ruling on faculty placements. Through appeals, the commission and the school district took the case to the state supreme court, which upheld the findings in September 1967. Most of the recommendations remained unfulfilled through the 1970s, as the commission had limited authority to enforce them.

Governor Scranton also supported the formation of an umbrella organization to solicit grassroots participation of resident constituents to reduce the immediate racial tensions in the aftermath of the demonstrations. The Greater Chester Movement (GCM) was formed with a mandate to unify and coordinate the efforts of existing government agencies and community organizations, including civil rights groups. The CFFN referred to the GCM as "a much needed moral face-lift after the city's real face was unmasked to reveal its grotesque features, distorted by injustice, bigotry, and decadence."[46] Branche was appointed the GCM's director of operations in 1965.

The mass protests and demonstrations of the civil rights movement came relatively early to Chester, prompting considerable attention from the national media and other activist organizations. For certain, Chester was not the only northern city to experience the sustained mass demonstrations, racial unrest, and police violence that accompanied the civil rights activism in the 1960s. Nor was it the only city where the debate over strategies and tactics split local organizations. That the 1964 protest campaign produced political and organizational costs for the local civil rights movement is to be expected. But in line with this book's argument that local power holders manipulate racial issues to effect changes for their own benefit, it is worth examining whether and to what degree those costs were influenced by the actions of Chester's white political establishment. The historical record points to questions about the relationship between Chester's political establishment and the CFFN during the protests of 1964 and immediately thereafter regarding the adoption of direct action as the key movement strategy, the extent of the tactics deployed, and the role of the CFFN leader Branche. Each of these points is taken in turn.

For the Old Guard activists Barbour and Raymond, the strategies adopted by Branche's CFFN meant the abandonment of legal efforts to use the courts to push desegregation or enforce desegregation orders. Barbour in particular considered it foolhardy to write off all whites as the opposition and continuously clamored for working with sympathetic whites to improve the civil rights situation.[47] Clearly, boycotts and sustained mass protests grabbed newspaper headlines and kept public attention focused on the issue of school desegregation. Few disputed the importance of such attention, but NAACP leaders, including leaders at the national office, questioned the practical implications of nightly protests and mass arrests. "The persistence of the demonstrations seems in part to have been designed to harass the police and to exploit a heightening emotional tension."[48] Old Guard leaders were puzzled and bothered by the CFFN's lack of an endgame or exit strategy. Branche fired up the young black population with demonstrations, pickets, and boycotts, but he offered few details about the movement's goals. Some repudiated their decades-long association, writing to the national NAACP in the heat of the unrest in March 1964 that they "[found] it impossible to accept the kind of leadership being manifested now and which has taken over this campaign."[49] Even Savage, the regional director who had once courted Branche and supported the CFFN, complained of Branche's uncompromising, if not outright obstructionist, attitude toward working with the NAACP or the Chester Human Relations Commission.

Branche engaged in one-upmanship with the established civil rights organizations in the community, boasting that the CFFN was the only true civil rights force in Chester. He cut the lines of communication with mediators and go-betweens in the white community. In open meetings that the press attended, he was prone to give ultimatums to city and school board officials, such as "do-or-die" deadlines for meeting demands. When the ultimatums were rejected or deemed impossible to satisfy, he walked out, held an impromptu press conference, and strongly condemned the other party. Such actions made a settlement of the school crisis that was agreeable to both blacks and whites less likely. In late March 1964 the school board accepted the Chester Human Relations Commission's call for a study of the feasibility of one large, central school to eliminate de facto segregation. The CFFN refused, insisting that the black leaders who would participate in the study no longer represented Chester's black community.[50] In April Branche announced that he would no longer deal with the Chester Human Relations Commission and would only meet directly with the entire school board. Mayor Gorbey arranged a meeting with Branche, the school board, and the white Chester Parents Association (CPA). Upon learning of the CPA's planned appearance at the meeting, Branche refused to attend.[51]

It is no surprise that the civil unrest of 1964 did not sit well with the majority of Chester and Delaware County whites. Angered by the costs of disruptions, downtown store owners and businesspeople pressed city hall with demands for restoration of law and order and welcomed the mass arrest of protesters. White customers opted to shop elsewhere. As the protests wore on and grew larger and the police response grew more aggressive, white residents feared the immediate and long-term repercussions of the end of their privileged place in the racial status quo. Parents demanded police protection of public schools and their mounting fears influenced the school board's decision to close all schools in April. The protests hardened the resolve of those committed to segregation. The CPA was formed after the November 1963 action at Franklin Elementary School and had grown to thirty-four hundred members by May 1964. "It was obvious that many white parents in Chester are deeply troubled by the new militancy of the city's Negro citizens and fearful that their children will be sent to strange schools in strange neighborhoods."[52] Those who could afford to do so transferred their children to parochial and private schools. Many expressed frustration with the city leaders' inability or unwillingness to end the unrest. Feeling abandoned by a political machine that had long preserved white privilege, hundreds left the city for the suburbs, where they were warmly welcomed (ironically) by the same political machine.

Not all white residents opposed the racial integration of public schools and an end to the social and political exclusion of Chester's black community. Many whites expressed an interest in working with black leaders either for reasons of social justice or pure pragmatism. But the NAACP-CFFN rift and the intransigence of Branche rendered co-operation among blacks and whites difficult. Branche canceled a number of planned meetings between CFFN leaders, the Chester Human Relations Commission, and the Chester School Board, prompting more protests and rallies. The Delaware County commissioners tried to organize a meeting with Chester city officials, the Chester School Board, the NAACP and CFFN leaders, and representatives of state and local human relations agencies. But the CFFN carried out a series of demonstrations at several Chester schools and public buildings the same day, prompting the school board to close all eighteen of Chester's public schools.[53]

The Chester School Board finally accepted a legal hearing—as Barbour and others prescribed—to allow a court to determine its role in ending de facto racial segregation, but complained of a lack of a single authoritative voice in the black community. At a meeting on April 17, 1964 Guy De Furia, the counsel for the school board, stated, "It's difficult for me to believe that the NAACP, an organization of that standard, refuses to go into court in a matter like this and would prefer to create turmoil and disorder in our city."[54] But the NAACP was powerless to do so. Branche's approach favored an end to communication with the white community. In April 1964 the question was posed at a board meeting: "Is there any responsible group who speaks for the Negro community? Who is the plaintiff in the court here? And I can't see any distinguishable, responsible group that anybody can deal with."[55] Conservative elements in the black civil rights movement questioned whether the strategy of direct action and official disengagement played into the hands of Republican politicians, a point noted by the Pennsylvania Human Rights Commission.

The two issues mentioned above would have amounted to very little but for the final, most important concern that Chester's civil rights community voiced—that of Branche's central role. In spite of the rankling within the NAACP and complaints about the CFFN leader's tactics and motivations, observers at the time conceded that nothing much would have happened in the Chester civil rights movement without Branche. But Branche had not created the conditions that brought thousands of Chester's black residents to the streets in protest; their discontent was decades in the making. Nor was he responsible for the growing unease and increased fear of whites over the impending demise (and comfort) of the city's racial status quo. The departure of whites for the suburbs may have accelerated after the unrest of 1964, but it had begun in earnest a decade earlier. But Branche was clearly a catalyst of events that led to significant changes in the black-white divide and the spatial order that upheld it. Even Raymond conceded, "We needed Stanley to light the fuse."[56]

During the summer of 1964, during the state Human Relations Commission's open hearings on Chester's school segregation, details about Branche's connections to the Republican machine began to emerge. Branche, it turns out, had spent some time in Chester prior to his reported arrival in 1962. In the spring of 1955 a Republican city councilman convinced him to work on an upcoming mayoral election. When he reappeared in Chester in 1962, it was widely reported that Branche became involved in the local civil rights struggle after his wife Ann Branche introduced him to Raymond. His wife had been raised in Chester by her aunt and uncle, the latter a prominent black lieutenant in McClure's Republican Party. Along the way to becoming the city's main civil rights leader, Stanley Branche had "cultivated a supposedly close friendship" with a local Republican magistrate. Through his earlier contacts with civil rights leaders in Maryland, Branche had become acquainted with Attorney General Robert Kennedy. In 1963 he accompanied the Republican Gorbey (who became Chester's mayor in 1964) to Kennedy's office to discuss Gorbey's possible appointment to a federal judgeship (it did not happen). The state Human Relations Commission heard testimony from McClure's operative at Sun Ship responsible for assisting the Pews' antiunionization efforts in the mid-1940s.[57] The commission learned that Branche was a "McClure plant" intentionally sent to infiltrate Chester's civil rights movement—not to uncover information (a network of machine lieutenants could easily have accomplished that) but for something far more nefarious: to stir up black discontent and instigate civil unrest that would provoke reaction from the white community. Apparently, McClure calculated that even Democrats fearful of urban unrest would flock to Republican candidates on Election Day. That failed to happen.[58] Raymond—who had long suspected that Branche was a McClure operative who routinely communicated details about civil right activities to machine officials—felt vindicated by such claims.[59]

With his appointment as director of operations with the GCM, suspicions regarding Branche's role in the civil rights unrest of 1964 and his motivations as an activist gathered further momentum. That appointment revealed the extent and depth of his connection to the Republican political machine. His former CFFN associates balked at his new position, calling his appointment an "insult to the Negro community and the Chester population at large."[60] "Many Negroes are wondering," penned a letter writer to the local newspaper, "if there are any 'power structure strings' attached to Stanley Branche's lucrative GCM salary."[61]

Branche once again resurfaced as an activist in the civil rights struggle in 1968, this time in Philadelphia, where he sided with the more radical elements in the Black Coalition, a short-lived multiracial action group formed in the wake of the assassination of Martin Luther King Jr. In the summer of 1968 the coalition sponsored dozens of large and small programs in Philadelphia's black neighborhoods, including reading programs, sports leagues, college placements, big sisters, and a children's aid society. Branche was appointed executive director, and from his West Philadelphia storefront office he spearheaded an adult job placement program that showed initial success in matching applicants with employers. His fiery rhetoric immediately won over many young followers and he did much to defuse tensions surrounding the Black Panthers convention held in the city in September 1968. But Branche's motives and leadership skills were soon questioned. The coalition grew alarmed at his ability to spend large sums of money and his lack of bill paying and financial record keeping. His appointment was terminated and the coalition disbanded in the fall of 1968.[62]

Whether or not McClure was directly responsible for stoking the embers of racial unrest, his political machine clearly benefited from its consequences. The spring of 1964 highlighted the differences between the city and its suburbs for Chester's whites who were still on the fence, considering a move. McClure and the Republican machine had already quietly constructed the political and economic supremacy of the sub-urbs, and the white exodus would only further consolidate the machine's power. McClure may have planted the activist Branche, but he com-manded neither the sequence of events of 1964 nor the sense of grass-roots achievement among black residents long silenced by the political workings of the machine.

McClure died on March 28, 1965. Whether or not he had intended to perpetrate race-baiting on such an organized and massive scale might never be fully known, but the answer is perhaps less important than the fact that his successors clearly capitalized on ensuing racial fears to fur-ther isolate Chester from the rest of the increasingly wealthy Delaware County. Thereafter many whites viewed Chester as a place of hostility and potential danger and a place to avoid.

An Opportunity to Move Forward: The Greater Chester Movement

Governor Scranton's direct intervention in the Chester crisis marked a pivotal turning point in the local civil rights movement. The timing of Scranton's commitment to address racism and poverty—especially his support for the GCM—coincided with the rollout of President Lyn-don B. Johnson's War on Poverty initiatives. The passage of the federal antipoverty Economic Opportunity Act of 1964 permitted cities to plan and implement comprehensive and coordinated approaches to solving pockets of entrenched poverty, such as black inner-city com-munities impoverished by various and lasting forms of institutional discrimination. In August 1964 the federal Office of Economic Opportunity designated the GCM as the Committee Action Agency in Delaware County to administer Johnson's War on Poverty programs.

The founding of the GCM in the wake of the unrest of 1964 provided a rare chance for local organizations to tap directly into emerging federal and state programs for poverty relief. The promise of the War on Poverty for grassroots change should not be underestimated. For the first time, the supremacy of Chester's local Republican machine politics could be bypassed. The GCM's core mission was to coordinate existing social services and determine means for delivery to the poorest residents at the block level.[63] Several mechanisms were designed to link agencies with residents. First, the organization formally networked with existing civil rights groups in Chester, including the NAACP, the local branch of CORE, the CFFN, the West End Minister's Fellowship, the Young Adult Council, and the Chester Civil Rights Committee. The GCM also created new block-level organizations and developed leadership training at the neighborhood level. Second, the city's poorest areas were divided into five geographic areas, each with its own social services coordinator who supervised block captains (four to each area) with direct links to residents. Coordinators worked with block captains to implement Community Action Projects centered on jobs, housing, and education. They organized volunteer work crews to paint houses, repair masonry, and fix or replace windows. In addition, the GCM opened Neighborhood Action Centers (NACs), storefront offices that functioned as a "casual drop-in center, handy, unpretentious, deliberately eschewing an air of officialdom, a bridge between the poor and existing aid programs."[64] NACs were intended as informal spaces that would build trust and "intimate rapport" between poor people and social service providers and government agencies. The staff served both as agents of city and county social services and as advocates for residents, "thereby increasing democratic participation in community government."[65] NACs organized meetings; programs on housing, credit unions, consumer cooperatives, employment, and business development; and elderly and youth programs.[66]

In 1965 the GCM received $1.5 million in funding from the federal government for the Jobs Corps program that led to the opening of the city's Opportunity Center, a combined educational and job skills training facility. The Adult Education and Vocational Education Divisions of the Chester School District also expanded their offerings through the GCM. Numerous occupational training courses, most of which were funded under the Manpower Development and Training Act, were offered through a cooperative program with the Pennsylvania State Employment Service.[67] The early efforts paid off. The GCM developed youth services and job programs with the help of General Electric, Scott Paper, and other local corporations.[68] The ability to keep a lid on further social unrest was attributed to the GCM as its most notable accomplishment.

Initially, the GMC appeared to offer Chester's poor minority residents a stake in grassroots political input, a means toward racial progress, and a path toward the alleviation of poverty. Such meaningful efforts at social change were short-lived, however. Its undoing was caused by a mix of national politics and inexorable pressures from Chester and Delaware County politicians to exert control. The GCM was one of hundreds of community action agencies tied to Johnson's War on Poverty. State and local social service programs worked directly with community activist organizations in poor minority districts in Philadelphia, New York, Cleveland, Buffalo, and many other cities, as statutorily required by federal policies aimed at maximizing representation and participation from the residents of affected communities. Federal antipoverty initiatives assumed that local institutions would have the motivation and capacity to design, support, and implement the necessary antipoverty programs. However, the grassroots response was not matched by an appropriate level of federal funding or oversight.[69] Many programs, including the GCM, were quickly beleaguered by the scope of community problems, lack of expertise, and overtaxed budgets.[70]

Within a year of its founding, the GCM was effectively hijacked by the Delaware County Republican political machine, which saw the organization as an easy front to funnel federal dollars into the pockets of political operatives. The GCM had sought to tap into leadership in the black community outside the influence of Chester politics, but local politics proved too resilient. The machine cleverly usurped the GCM's mission and provided "expertise" for managing the War on Poverty. The GCM's grassroots origins faded and block-level volunteers with direct access to their neighbors were distanced from policy making. As the next chapter details, the GCM became one of several institutional mechanisms implicated in the establishment of a parasitic economy in the inner city.

From Containment to Fear

In the early 1960s the strategic employment of race in Chester transitioned. At the start of the decade, the racial social and spatial order in which blacks were separately and unequally contained was already under pressure from demographic and economic changes enveloping the region. By the close of 1964 the framing of the racial divide by whites and white institutions had shifted toward a focus on the menace posed by black efforts toward social justice. This new narrative of the ghetto as a threatening space to be feared by whites proved useful to local stakeholders in urban change for decades to come.

The repeated standard history of the civil rights movement rightfully emphasizes the struggle of black Americans for equal treatment and fair access to social, political, and economic opportunities. The Chester story is no different. However, the collective endeavors of the city's poor and disenfranchised inspired a perverse secondary function that facilitated urban changes benefiting those with capital, power, and privilege. This second, duplicitous function, based entirely on deception and the raw abuse of power, by no means detracts from the significance and meaning of mobilization and resistance for the thousands of Chester residents who participated in protests and demonstrations. But it is a clear, albeit unusual, example of how misshapen ideas and accepted wisdom of the racial divide enabled and arguably accelerated urban transformation. For many whites, the civil unrest of 1964 solidified the suburban option as not only ideal, but as a solution that was urgently necessary and incriminated the city as a space to fear.

For a city suffering from the consequences of entrenched institution-alized racism, the founding of the GCM afforded an opportunity as a truly grassroots force for social change. The opportunity was squandered. Under the guise of providing assistance to the city's poor and addressing patterns of racial discrimination, the Delaware County political machine marshaled its network of resources to transform the GCM into a money-peddling enterprise rewarding faithful political operatives. The GCM's origin as a grassroots solution to racial discrimination provided racial cover for a new, post–civil rights local politics of disinvestment and extraction of urban resources. As the following chapter details, the pilfering of the GCM was the first of several incidences in which local elites used the prevailing rhetoric of race and racism as a means to profit from and reinforce control over poor minorities. The result was more of the same—disappointment and fatalism among Chester's dwindling population.

Five Square Miles of Hell

After the civil unrest of 1964 and the early efforts of the GCM to address discrimination and poverty at the neighborhood level, the racial divisions in Chester only worsened, relegating the city's poor black residents to more concentrated poverty and, as this chapter examines, greater vulnerability to political and economic exploitation at the hands of elites. Ongoing segregation at the metropolitan level clearly furthered the isolation of poor blacks in the inner city. Whites and later, working- and middle-class blacks, left the city, along with industries, employment opportunities, and economic capital. Those who either chose to stay or were simply left behind were faced with few sustainable prospects for the improvement in living conditions.[1] Strong social traditions in older black communities were challenged and weakened, as residents faced withering neighborhood ties, declining civic organizations, and the closing of locally owned small businesses. In their place emerged a largely informal subsistence economy in which many residents were compelled to participate as a means of economic survival. By the late 1970s the racial divide between city and suburb was effectively a class divide as well, with the inner city home to an increasing number of jobless and economically deprived people and the suburbs the domain of both the working and the middle classes.

But it would be a mistake to assume that the city of the post–civil rights era was shaped exclusively by ongoing segregation, institutional decline, and the heightened exodus of whites and middle-class blacks. Contrary to the idea of the inner city as abandoned and left to its own devices, where residents themselves develop their own illicit economy and dysfunctional social organizations as a means of survival, Chester was not spared the intentional pilfering and theft of its limited resources by politically connected elites. Alongside the steady disinvestment of economic and social capital grew a sophisticated parasitic economy of vice and criminal activity controlled by white power holders and black political operatives but shouldered by the city's black population. Indeed, not only were black residents the intended targets of Chester's parasitic economy that worsened already precarious living conditions, but they were also explicitly portrayed in the media and popular discourse as the cause of urban crime, as both violators and beneficiaries of the rampant lawlessness that overtook the city in the 1980s and 1990s.

The vast public discourse and rhetoric fixated on black individual and cultural deficiencies did not simply coincide with the structural forces that contributed to advanced ghettoization. It stood and arguably still stands as an alternative explanation for inner-city poverty and urban social problems. Racial stigma fixates on particular destructive behaviors that not only comprise an exaggerated depiction of an entire population, but also bleed over as an explanation for a host of inner-city problems from chronic unemployment to abandoned, trash-strewn lots. The prominence accorded to "cultural deficiencies" in majority-black neighborhoods contributes to the pervasive understanding of Chester as a threatening space, a city to be avoided. In turn, the racial stigma of the inner city proves useful to local elites as cover for a host of officially sanctioned, profitable, and illicit activities. Stigmatization facilitates a post–civil rights parasitic economy based on the pilfering of the inner-city built environment and more importantly, the residents who live there.

As this chapter shows, the racial stigmatization of Chester provided reliable cover for various forms of officially sanctioned vice and corruption, as the social problems caused by such activities were effortlessly attributed to the cultural lifestyles of poor minority residents. Already reeling from segregation and a vulnerable class position, Chester residents felt the added sting of racial stereotypes readily deployed as the underlying cause of the city's woes. Perversely, the much maligned and hyped "ghetto life"—served up as the reason for urban decline—proves to be more the product of public policies and private sector practices.

Racial stigma damaged the collective capacity of Chester residents to oppose, let alone formulate an alternative to the parasitic urban underdevelopment that characterized much of the city's political economy during the 1980s and 1990s.

Plundering Antipoverty Initiatives

The initial architecture underlying federal antipoverty schemes favored community-based organizations and grassroots involvement in program implementation. On the heels of protracted civil rights demonstrations and the state's ensuing intervention to address racial segregation and poverty, the likelihood of real progress in education, housing, and overall circumstances for Chester's black community seemed high in the summer of 1964. The early months of Chester's neighborhood-based demonstration program, the GCM, were a test of 1960s antipoverty efforts, weaving together grassroots participation, social welfare institutions, and state and federal assistance tied to the War on Poverty. In the fall of 1964 the GCM opened its first NAC in the West End, the city's largest black community. Several others opened in storefronts across the poor neighborhoods by year's end. GCM workers provided aid and assistance to individuals and families with housing and rent issues, utility bills, emergency food, and referrals to city and county social welfare agencies. In 1965 the state funded child day care centers and a combined federal-state-city grant funded the development of a citywide public library system.

Yet the potential for sustained improvements in poverty relief and racial relations was short-lived. As mentioned in the last chapter, the local political machine quickly swallowed up the GCM, becoming a front for controlling the increasing amount of state and federal funds linked to the War on Poverty. Community organizers, social service workers, and residents leveled charges of political favoritism, patronage, and foot-dragging on implementing anticipated changes at the neighborhood level. In the fall of 1967 the federal Office of Economic Opportunity investigated the GCM's operations, including the role of Chester's mayor as a member of the GCM steering committee. In February 1969 the GCM's steering committee chairman, Kenneth L. Smith (the head of the Department of Christian Ethics at Crozer Theological Seminary), resigned and leveled a number of serious criticisms about the GCM's operations. These included a lack of adequate internal bookkeeping and record keeping, the manipulation of jobs and money by GCM officials, and directives to community action centers' employees not to actively assist in organizing poor residents or the GCM would face criticism from local politicians. Field workers were allegedly told to "stay at their desks and out of the ghetto."[2]

By the end of the 1960s Delaware County's white elites had successfully turned the GCM into a modernized version of the city's early twentieth-century patronage and loyalty machine. By the time the GCM program ended in 1976, its structure and operation mirrored McClure's system of handpicking and rewarding lieutenants positioned within the city's black communities for block-level discipline and maintenance of a post–civil rights political and racial status quo. During the height of the War on Poverty, when federal and state agencies were funding programs to better inner-city employment training, housing, welfare, and education, the core function of the GCM was to funnel those dollars as rewards in a network of loyal operatives and maintain (or allow to worsen) the conditions of black poverty to remain eligible for the flow of public subsidies. At every turn, resident petitions for improvements in housing, education, and community services disappeared into a bureaucracy managed by black political operatives beholden to maintaining the status quo. As the public "face" of the GCM was increasingly staffed by black machine operatives, the city could point to the organization as evidence of community self-empowerment and self-governance; thus any shortcomings of the effectiveness of the GCM could not be the result of discriminatory staff hiring.

In 1972 the *Delaware County Daily Times* published a monthlong exposé that revealed the extent of the GCM's political favoritism, nepotism, and reward system for the loyalty and patronage of local operatives on the ground. The newspaper's staff reviewed hundreds of documents and conducted interviews with residents, businesspeople, civic leaders, and past and present GCM employees. The paper concluded that the county's Republican Party "pulls the strings for the local war on poverty" and found that little of the $12.4 million in federal and state aid the GCM received between 1964 and 1972 was used to assist Chester's poor residents.[3] Nepotism was extensive in the GCM, with top administrators creating positions for spouses and other relatives or hiring them to fill vacancies.[4] Representatives of the business community, such as the Chester Small Businessmen's Association, populated the top GCM committees. Officials favored purchasing goods and services from known business associates or, in some cases, from companies in which they owned an outright interest. The GCM's day care center was housed in a building rented for $1,500 a month, "three times the going commercial real estate rent," from a real estate firm owned by a board member's relative.[5] In 1972 the day care center employed twenty-seven workers, many of whom were spouses of GCM committee members, but enrolled only twenty-two students.[6] The owner of an insurance firm that received $22,000 in premiums from the GCM between 1968 and 1970 was a member of its steering committee at the same time, and the mayor appointed him to the GCM board in 1971.[7] The Opportunity Center, in its origins, was successful. Hundreds attended training programs in vocational skills and General Educational Development (GED) courses. By 1969 most of the professional training staff had departed and by 1972 its advisory board had been disbanded, reducing the number and quality of training programs.[8]

The political appointment of black operatives in the GCM assured a measure of discipline and control at the organization's point of contact with the city's neediest residents. A key black lieutenant in the local Republican political machine oversaw a range of hiring, from custodians to the director of the Opportunity Center. He also served as chairman of the Housing Development Corporation of Chester, an agency partly funded by the GCM and partly by the city, and his wife was employed at the day care center. From its founding, the most progressive component of the GCM were the NACs, the grassroots liaisons between poor people and government agencies. By 1969 the storefronts were understaffed and opened intermittently. As residents' complaints were rarely addressed, the number of clients and visitors dropped. The politically inclined GCM leadership informally instructed NAC employees to discourage collective action by low-income residents. The *Daily Times* reporting noted, "Any grassroots protests of poverty conditions are systematically smothered by the political establishment, further hampering the action center's effectiveness."[9] The *Daily Times* investigation concluded:

> A combination of the Republican organization's aggressiveness and black apathy has enabled the politically inclined to take control of the GCM. Political domination appears to be a principal cause for the GCM's failure in the war on poverty. On paper, the GCM is beautifully divided between one-third public sector, one-third private sector, and one-third low-income neighborhood; in practice GCM is at the beck and call of City Hall. The GOP has stacked the deck in its favor by infiltrating people into the private and low-income categories.[10]

The reaction to the newspaper's investigation was both predictable and revealing. Most of Chester's blacks had long considered the GCM an arm of city hall and the Republican organization. Its key players were, after all, familiar faces in the local political machine. Once hopeful, residents, church leaders, and remaining civil rights activists were resigned to the reality that the GCM was ineffective and that it had become another institution that appeared to help people but functioned only to repress them. Black operatives lambasted the *Daily Times* investigation, pointing to the GCM's few tangible results and portraying the organization as run by and for the black community. County and city government officials charged that the newspaper's reporters spoke with a small, disaffected segment of the black community and that the GCM otherwise was delivering services to the city's neediest. The everyday conditions in black neighborhoods suggested otherwise.

In July and August 1968 the Pennsylvania Human Relations Commission held investigatory hearings on the state of poverty and race relations in Chester. Its findings showed that after four years of GCM operations little had changed. Over one-third of the city's black families received welfare assistance. In 1968 the unemployment rate for blacks was 16 percent, over twice that for whites at 7 percent. The majority of Chester's black residents continued to live in overcrowded segregated neighborhoods in poorly maintained multifamily housing units owned by absentee landlords, whites who had left the city for the suburbs and continued to own and rent city property.[11] The commission labeled the housing in neighborhoods where the majority of blacks resided substandard. Housing units operated by the CHA fared no better. Nearly complete racial segregation of public housing persisted in 1968, with all 350 units in Lamokin Village and 390 units in the Ruth L. Bennett Homes occupied by blacks and 100 percent of McCaffery Village white.[12] The commission found that the CHA intentionally actively maintained racial segregation of its projects, creating "established permanent communities of the economically disadvantaged; [that] become permanent hearts for ghettos in microcosm; and have been administered in such an aura of paternalism to have fostered the antipathies of tenants and adjacent residents and business operators alike."[13]

The commission found racial discrimination pervasive across all city services and agencies, from its grassroots antipoverty initiatives and housing authority to its police force, urban redevelopment agency, and school district. Its report also concluded that the GCM's activities in connection with these services and agencies aided official racial segregation and therefore sustained high poverty levels. It cited the testimonies of residents as evidence of vast inequalities in service provision, from fire and ambulance services to trash collection and public safety, between black and white neighborhoods. White neighborhoods and certain small areas within black districts were "politically favored" in the patronage system of the municipal administration. "The failure of the City Administration to take affirmative action to provide redress of complaint under the aegis of law assuring true equality of opportunity," the commission's report noted, "has been a major factor in the deepening of thus-far unchecked racial antipathies and the very apparent racial polarization in the City of Chester."[14]

Black Poverty Pays

Chester's post–civil rights urban politics of extraction and disinvestment was not limited to the white-dominated power structure siphoning off state and federal dollars intended to alleviate the city's racially inflected unemployment, poverty, and poor housing. Indeed, local politicians and affiliated business partners brazenly harnessed networks to profit from their own creation of an insalubrious parallel economy based on embezzlement and extortion at the hands of poor black residents. The prevailing and sustained racialized narrative of Chester as a black, poor, and increasingly dangerous city enabled this system of corruption to operate and flourish. As such, many of the city's woes directly attributable to official systematic corruption were instead readily and effortlessly blamed on the culture and way of life of its black residents.

Operational changes in Delaware County's ruling political machine partly enabled the visceral turn to outright corruption, usury, and exploitation in Chester. As pointed out in prior chapters, the longevity of the Republican Party political machine was testament to its organizational discipline and rigid and effective authority structure. For as long as the Republican machine controlled Chester and Delaware County's political and judicial administrations, the structure of patronage was hierarchical and orderly, from a War Board that managed countywide decisions that affected thousands to the individual traffic officer writing a parking ticket. Half a decade after McClure's death and with the shift in political focus from the city to the county fully in place, the system of patronage was no longer nearly as organized and rationalized. It devolved into localism and extremism fraught with risky ventures of party captains hell-bent on exploiting as much gain and monetary profit as possible from the declining city.

As the machine decentralized and party discipline evaporated, the organization of Chester's politics took on a more obvious parasitic and extractive character. Municipal corruption was endemic in the decline of many older industrial cities. But Chester's formal and institutional embrace of corruption was aided by the remnants of the former machine's patronage system that incentivized the participation of black party leaders in the everyday operation of white rule and economic exploitation. Through the course of the 1970s and 1980s the associations and networks comprised of local white and black politicians; the administrations of police, courts, social welfare, and housing; and the local branches of organized crime and gambling and narcotics syndicates were laid bare, transforming Chester into a frontier town of crime, vice, and official corruption and its residents into hostages to costly schemes endorsed by parasitic urban politics.

Corruption involved large sums of money and the abuse of power at high levels of municipal administration. But it also involved low-level schemes that targeted Chester's economically vulnerable black residents. In doing so, official corruption relied on and reproduced prevailing racial discourses that associated black inner cities with criminality, discourses that popularly defined the urban-suburban divide in the post–civil rights era. In 1971 a Pennsylvania Crime Commission investigation found that a system of organized kickbacks targeting black residents prevailed throughout Delaware County's criminal justice system. Unscrupulous bail bondsmen colluded with district judges to uniformly set unnecessarily high bail for low-level criminal offenses. Under this setup, individuals (young black males) arrested for minor infractions such as loitering were charged with and arraigned for more serious crimes. The trumped-up charges triggered setting bail when it was not needed, requiring defendants (and their families) to secure bail. The inflated bail costs provided a substantial premium for the bondsman, and both district justices and police officers shared the proceeds as a kick-back. Charges were later reduced or dropped.

The favored inner circle of bail bondsmen had direct connections to city hall and officials in the Chester Police Department. All were white with the exception of Melvin Wade, a black building supply agent who became a professional bondsman in 1969. During the hearings of the Pennsylvania Crime Commission, Wade provided elaborate testimony on the operations of Chester's corrupt bail system. He explained how white bondsmen accessed arraigned defendants through contacts, ar-ranged through the mayor's office, with top police officials and magis-trates. Wade's bail scam was more grassroots. He cultivated relationships with individual police lieutenants and captains whom he "tipped" for notification of arrests. Wade gradually cornered a small share of the Chester bail bond business. In the course of the investigation, the com-mission also learned of improper activities surrounding zoning building permits and municipal contracts and financial kickbacks in municipal purchases.[15]

The bail kickback operation was systematic. The division of payoffs required routine coordination of the local judiciary, police, and bail bondsmen. The vast majority of its victims were black residents and disproportionately young black males. In its review of the records of Chester district justices, the Crime Commission found high arrest rates for blacks for summary offenses such as disorderly conduct and breach of the peace, which were technically noncriminal and punishable by a fine.[16] The entire system operated under the cover of racial rhetoric and images that assigned large parts of the city as crime-ridden and its black residents as criminally culpable or at best, permissive and party to a culture of illegality.

A series of Crime Commission investigations conducted in the 1970s found evidence of a city awash in a number of sanctioned illegal activi-ties, including gambling, prostitution, narcotics, loan sharking, official bribery, kickbacks, and payoffs. All these enterprises siphoned money from federal and state dollars to residents' pocket change, out of Chester.

In each case, city hall's involvement was extensive. Two black Republican Party committee members, Frank Miller and Herman Fontaine, ran an elaborate illegal numbers racket made possible by their political connections and regular payoffs to high-ranking police and local government officials, including Chester's mayor. Both had served on the board of the Delaware County Citizen Coalition (CITCO), a GCM venture created to jump-start small manufacturing businesses that would provide employment to black laborers. Funded by federal dollars and administered by several black party officials, CITCO closed after three years and a single failed pilot program, citing "management problems and lack of experience."[17] The GCM funneled thousands of dollars to a nightclub owned by the two for a daytime cultural enrichment program for Chester's black youth. GCM officials defended the expense and the choice of the nightclub, stating "it was one of the few places with suitable facilities that would accept a party of black children."[18]

A three-year Crime Commission investigation outlined the details of the Miller-Fontaine gambling enterprise. The numbers racket employed over one hundred employees and grossed between $8 million and $11 million annually. They used the profits to purchase corner stores, warehouses, restaurants, bars, and other small businesses in Chester to serve as fronts for the expanding numbers racket and for payoffs to police and high-level city officials.[19] While running the enterprise, both Miller and Fontaine continued as operatives for the Republican Party.[20] The commission noted that the extent of the successful operation and its ability to continue unabated were made possible only by ties with Chester's government. The police provided immunity from arrest for numbers writers and fended off competition by selectively arresting other non-sanctioned numbers writers.[21] Yet despite months of commission hearings during the three-year investigation, no officials were charged. In 1974 a Delaware County special prosecutor issued a report in which he stated, "It would be well to emphasize at this point in this report that at the close of the Crime Commission's investigation no evidence suitable for prosecution was turned over to any local, state, or national prosecution agency and in its April 1973 Report the Crime Commission stated that it had no evidence to back up any of its charges."[22]

In 1975 county Democrats pressured a Philadelphia special prosecutor to look anew at the Crime Commission reports and findings and demand that the county's special prosecutor turn over crucial documents that could lead to prosecutions.[23] In response, the U.S. attorney's office launched a criminal investigation into official corruption in Chester. Four years later Mayor Nacrelli was convicted of accepting kickbacks from gamblers under the Racketeer Influenced and Corrupt Organizations (RICO) statute of the Organized Crime Control Act of 1970. He was sentenced to six years in prison.[24] After his federal conviction and while awaiting imprisonment in a federal facility, Nacrelli continued as chairman of the Republican Party, screening job applicants for the Comprehensive Employment Training Act program to determine their political affiliations and placing nonprofessional patronage employees in the Chester Upland School District.[25]

The federal case against Nacrelli detailed the extent to which the city government of Chester operated as an institutional means of extortion and systematic extraction of resources and capital from residents and legitimate businesses. Government revenues were largely used to pay for the silence of municipal employees, while top officials skimmed profits from vast illegal enterprises. Any internal inquiries into employee misconduct or questionable governmental expenditures were handled swiftly by immediate dismissal and employment blacklisting. Uniformed police officers were "no more than submissive pawns in the game being played by organized gamblers and corrupt politicians in Chester."[26] Little changed after Nacrelli's conviction. The former mayor served two years of his federal prison sentence, all the while overseeing operations in Chester. According to a Pennsylvania Crime Commission report, Nacrelli quickly resumed full control of party operations upon his release from prison and return to Chester. He continued to select employees for patronage jobs in municipal offices, the Chester Upland School District, the CHA, and the Chester Redevelopment Authority.

He routinely convened backroom meetings with members of the Chester City Council without notifying (or inviting) the mayor.

The city's downward spiral continued through the late 1970s and the 1980s fueled by newer, high-tech forms of vice and graft directly tied to the municipal administration and in turn, the region's white political system. Video poker replaced the numbers racket. Rampant narcotics trafficking led to syndicate and gang turf wars and street crime. Chester emerged as a central stopping point in the trafficking of cocaine and heroin between southern Florida and New York City.

The city's segregated public housing developments functioned as open-air drug markets in the 1980s. This in itself was not unique. Many housing projects across the country had become turf for drug dealers, and several cities sought to limit drug activities through community policing and police cooperation with tenant associations. However, Chester was different. City hall sanctioned a hands-off policy in which the police avoided the drug-plagued housing projects, most notably William Penn Homes. Ignored by law enforcement, William Penn Homes became the one-stop hub for cocaine and heroin distribution, sales, and open consumption. In her testimony to the Pennsylvania Crime Commission, Mayor Willie Mae Leake testified that when she became mayor in 1986, she had to instruct the police to return to public housing developments. Her predecessor advised her otherwise, telling her: "When I was mayor, I told them to stay out of the William Penn project. . . . After all, those people don't pay taxes and they don't vote."[27]

The Pennsylvania Crime Commission convened once again in 1990 and issued a statement that spelled out the constellation of factors contributing to the city's decades-long reputation for official corruption and rampant criminal activity: "As Chester's industry further declined, as federal social services, especially labor training, disappeared and the local municipal and county governments abandoned the idea of salvaging the inner city (and instead embarked on draining it of resources and capital), the drug informal economy and associated social organization flourished."[28] In making an explicit connection between the parasitic

The legacy of urban extraction.

political economy and the city's decline and numerous social problems, the commission recognized Chester's predicament as the willful consequence of politics and urban policy.

The dynamics of a post–civil rights race strategy enabled and legitimized a cynical politics of parasitism, corruption, and extraction. First, the appearance of Chester's self-determined governance facilitated ongoing official corruption and criminality. The practice of incorporating black political leaders and black functionaries into white-dominated county-based party rule provided racial cover for corruption and vice. The political machine was smaller and broken up into minifiefdoms (of which Chester was one), but it did not cede the city to black control. Instead, white party officials handpicked dependable black leaders to provide a veneer of black self-governance and political control, enabling what the Crime Commission called an "interracial, criminal alliance."[29] All the while, the white power holders ruled over an organized corrupt system that was picking through the remains of a city largely left behind. Local government oversaw corruption of the petty and the grand sorts, skimming off the top of federal funds for social programs and fleecing the city's poorest residents of their limited incomes. The parasitic political economy in Chester thrived against a steadily worsening social and economic backdrop that rendered the city particularly vulnerable to criminal exploitation and cynical political manipulation.

Second, the regional racial dynamics of black inner cities and white suburbs sustained the illusion that the desperate situations of cities like Chester were caused by the residents themselves. By the mid-1990s most residents of the Philadelphia region considered Chester a dangerous place, one to avoid. Negative news stories fueled the oversimplified story of an exodus of white residents and the rise of a minority-ruled hotbed for criminals and welfare recipients. In short, Chester was written off and made invisible save for profiteers of corruption and vice. Caught in the midst of declines in public safety, education, and other social services, Chester's post-Nacrelli leaders turned to private sources to spearhead even the most modest form of urban redevelopment and offer some promise of replenishing bare city coffers. As the following discussion suggests, Chester became receptive, if not vulnerable, to particularly opportunistic forms of private sector investment—environmental waste.

Chasing Smokestacks: One Black, One White

Chester's local political leaders intentionally housed waste disposal facilities in the city as a form of urban economic development, but this was not unique. Other poor northeastern cities facing the economic burden of deindustrialization did so as well. Most waste-to-energy facilities built in the 1980s and 1990s, for example, were constructed in defunct industrial zones in poor cities. Chester followed suit, opening a trash-to-steam incinerator operated by the Westinghouse Corporation in 1991. What is unique to the Chester case is the clustering of four additional waste facilities in the same privately owned parcel along the Delaware River adjacent to a low-income, primarily black residential neighborhood.

Between 1986 and 1991 the strategic politics of race inundated the contested process of siting an incinerator in the city's West End. The siting process unfolded as a protracted and highly public conflict between the city's first black mayor and the county's white political establishment—or so it would seem. The appearance of political discord over the city's waste zone actually reveals how key stakeholders wielded discourses of racial subordination to push through extensive plans for toxic economic development. The wielding (or use) of rhetoric of race and racism was an effective political strategy precisely because it tapped into the experiences of discrimination that many residents of Chester's West End faced. As the following account shows, issues of race and racism were deployed in manifold ways, transparent, obscure, and even bizarre. A rhetoric of race and racism shaped and ultimately concealed the decision on how many incinerators would be built, where they would be sited, who would own and operate them, and who would benefit or lose in the long run. Wielding the rhetoric of race and racism proved highly pragmatic and profitable for Delaware County's proincinerator faction but not for the minority residents of Chester.

During his imprisonment and after, Nacrelli retained control over most of the city's business, from securing bids and contracts to approving all political appointments. In 1986 his former secretary, Leake, became the first black mayor of Chester. By the time Leake took office, Delaware County political leaders had partnered with a private firm to incinerate trash from all its forty-nine municipalities. The county raised $300 million to construct a trash-to-steam plant through a bond issue underwritten by the Pittsburgh conglomerate Russell, Rea, and Zappala (RR&Z) and Bear, Stearns, and Company Inc. of New York. In 1985 RR&Z formed Chester Solid Waste Associates to purchase waterfront land and develop a megawaste park where the county's incinerator, a medical waste incinerator, and other waste facilities could be built. The county plan allowed Westinghouse to build, manage, and own the waste-to-steam plant and to guarantee disposal of 465,000 tons of the county's trash each year for twenty-five years. The plan approved a facility with a burn capacity twice as large that need to incinerate the county's trash.[30] As negotiations moved forward, Westinghouse was permitted to seek waste disposal contracts from municipal governments in Delaware and New Jersey.[31] Nacrelli helped broker the county's deal with RR&Z and Westinghouse.

Within months of taking office, Mayor Leake announced that Chester would build its own waste disposal facility as the cornerstone of the city's plan for economic revitalization. Leake envisioned Chester as a "waste magnet" profiting from packed landfills and looming trash crises in larger nearby cities such as Philadelphia and New York. When Philadelphia's proposal to build its own municipal trash incinerator was defeated in the early planning stages, Leake saw the opportunity for Chester to economically benefit from burning trash. In October 1986 Chester officials secured a verbal agreement for a multiyear contract to dispose of Philadelphia's trash. Leake's planned incinerator would dispose of trash not only from Philadelphia but also from the towns and suburbs of the tri-state area. The proposed waste-to-energy facility would process forty-eight hundred tons of garbage a day, burning 50 percent, recycling around 30 percent, and shipping the remaining residual material to a landfill. It would generate an estimated sixty-six megawatts of electricity a day or about the amount used by sixty-six thousand households.

The mayor and other Chester officials launched an aggressive public relations campaign to build the incinerator. Leake promoted the incinerator as the best opportunity for the city to secure its own economic development; its $335 million cost should be considered an investment in Chester's future. The incinerator would generate between $5 million to $10 million a year from tipping fees (the fee per tonnage of trash from municipalities) and the sale of the electricity generated, three hundred new jobs with a minimum of 25 percent of the workforce minority employees, and up to one thousand additional jobs in new firms locating in Chester to buy and sell recyclable materials.[32]

The mayor's economic message struck a chord with the residents of a city suffering from high unemployment, fiscal debt, and few development opportunities. The city's special counsel for the project called the incinerator "the cornerstone of the city's economic development program."[33] An influential local Baptist minister (and former local NAACP president) equated the plan with salvation and summoned Chester citizens to support it. "We are down on our knees and we need to be picked up. This project could bring us back to the good days. We will be able to stand on our own feet."[34] As the first black mayor with strong ties in the city's black civic community, Leake appeared to be a fighter with Chester's best interests at heart. A *Philadelphia Inquirer* profile on the mayor noted her popularity among residents, many of whom attributed a messianic quality to her conviction to lead Chester to economic recovery. The article quoted Leake as saying: "Somehow God is going to help me or show me the way to change the course of Chester. And I pray, I believe it will happen."[35] Since the mayor's efforts focused exclusively on job creation and economic redemption, her public relations campaign did not address any potential environmental or health concerns of a waste incinerator located within the city.[36]

Leake's promises of Chester's economic revitalization seemed convincing, but the incinerator plan was troubled from the start. Delaware County's plan for its waste incinerator already had a site and funding in place. Lacking both, the city started with a clear disadvantage and never recovered. In addition, the county took advantage of its head start and thwarted its competitor's efforts at every chance. Over the next eighteen months, significant challenges to the plant's financing and siting emerged and quickly escalated.[37] In August 1986 the securities firm handling the city's tax-exempt bonds dropped out, citing concerns about the project's feasibility. The firm specifically mentioned the city's inability to secure a site to build the incinerator and no guaranteed commitment for a steady source of trash. Within a week Matthews and Wright, a Wall Street investment firm, signed on to the deal and hastily purchased the bonds on August 29, two days before federal tax oversight regulations were to change. The regulations in place prior to September 1 allowed the $335,000 tax-exempt bond to be issued before the funds were actually needed for construction expenses. The terms of the bond sale, however, fixed the timing of the Chester project, as it required either full repayment or the plant's completion by August 1991.[38]

The city's last-minute bond sale raised enough suspicions to warrant a federal securities fraud investigation. In 1987 investigators alleged that Matthews and Wright had used a fictitious bank to create a paper transfer of $1.7 billion in bonds for Chester and other distressed cities, issued just before the key tax deadline.[39] Mayor Leake dismissed concerns that the charges would jeopardize the incinerator funding, describing the firm as "sympathetic to the plight of poor, black cities like Chester."[40] In 1991 the U.S. Internal Revenue Service (IRS) informed the city that its bond issue did not comply with requirements for tax-exempt status. The IRS determined that Chester's bonds were actually sold two months after the September 1, 1986, deadline for tax-exempt status.[41] A Matthews and Wright official and a consultant were indicted on fifty-two federal counts of fraud, bribery, and conspiracy, and a bond lawyer pleaded guilty to a charge of failing to report a felony.[42]

Chester's financing problems were matched by its failure to acquire a location to build the incinerator. Shortly after the mayor announced the August bond funding, Delaware County officials thwarted the city's plant location plan. In September the county council voted to purchase the city's intended site for $1 from the Delaware County Economic Development Center Inc., a nonprofit county agency that had bought the land from Reynolds Aluminum in 1980. When asked about the reason for the purchase, the Delaware County councilman leading the county's incinerator plan noted "the questionable status of Chester's plan."[43] Four days later the Delaware County Council diverted $280,000 in Community Development Block Grant funds originally earmarked for Chester to pay for maintenance costs of the newly purchased industrial park. Determined to move forward, the city condemned and announced plans to take possession of a large waterfront parcel owned by Philadelphia

Electric in October. But the utility firm was in negotiations to purchase the electricity that would be generated once the county's Westinghouse incinerator came online. Philadelphia Electric waged a legal battle over the city's condemnation and possession that continued past the city's bond-imposed deadline of 1991.[44]

As the city-county conflict widened, Chester politicians and local supporters cast the battle over the incinerators as a fight for the city's independence from imperious county rule and eventually as a racial issue pitting the majority black city against the white suburbs. Race and racism, then, entered the lexicon of the siting process not as an issue of the racially disproportionate impact of environmental hazards but as a means to advance one incinerator plan over another. In the closing weeks of 1986 Delaware County political leaders and some Chester city council members urged the mayor to acknowledge the growing obstacles and the increasing improbability that the waste-to-steam incinerator plan would be built. A former mayor, who had vacated the office to become county sheriff, publicly counseled Leake to strike a compromise deal with the county. Leake's strategy was to buy time. In order for the county's incinerator to be built, the city would need to sign a host agreement. The county offered a $2 million signing fee. Westinghouse promised the city $2.4 million once the environmental permits were approved and an additional $2 million in payments in 1988 and in 1989. The company also pledged $2.40 per ton of trash handled, which amounted to $2.35 million a year if the plant were to operate at full capacity.

Leake refused, claiming, "We're being coerced." Leveling charges of interference and political foul play, the mayor claimed that the county profited from keeping Chester economically depressed and that her plans for economic autonomy threatened the historical imbalance between the city and the county.[45] Leo Bean, the city-appointed special representative for the incinerator project, also cast the dispute with the county as one of local rule and economic autonomy: "Chester is on the brink of economic rebirth and it needs to control its own destiny." Bean continued: "Chester has been under the absolute control of the county for years. The county says we will take care of you, we will give you what you need, the scraps. . . . It's time that the county recognizes the city has problems, severe problems, and putting a trash-to-steam plant there is not going to solve the problems. It's just going to make a private developer rich and get the county's trash processed for free."[46] The rhetoric of the city-county conflict took a decidedly racial tone as the prospects for moving the incinerator plan forward continued to dwindle in 1987. In a high-stakes effort to find a new site for the incinerator, Leake asked the residents of Chester's majority black West End neighborhood to "sacrifice" their homes.[47] The city proposed taking 248 homes, 50 vacant lots, and 7 businesses on 22 acres along the waterfront. All the homes and businesses would have to be demolished after lengthy negotiations with the individual property owners. On the evening of June 30, 1987 Leake made a public appeal to about 125 residents at Calvary Baptist Church. According to the *Philadelphia Inquirer*, Leake first calmed the skeptical crowd, telling them: "As I entered tonight, I saw some very unhappy faces. Remember that I'm here for your benefit, not to hurt you." To build her case for the residents' consent, the mayor reminded the audience of the importance of the incinerator as the best and last chance to address the city's poverty, high crime rate, and declining tax base. The church's minister (and the mayor's most ardent supporter) furthered the appeal, telling those gathered, "Finally we get somebody in the mayor's office who wants to stand up and bring the city back, and if you care about our children and our city, there has to be a sacrifice."[48]

Leake made a personal appeal for racial solidarity with the predominantly black crowd, declaring that "as a black woman she had their best interests at heart." As the *Inquirer* reported, her words appeared to work. "The crowd stood and joined hands and prayed with the mayor. Then the residents, many of whom were angry at the meeting's onset, walked over to shake the mayor's hand, kiss her cheek and wish her good luck with the project." One of the residents, a retired schoolteacher, spoke to the crowd: "I'm for anything that will help Chester. I'm willing to give up my house that I've lived in since I was 9 months old." As many applauded, she turned to the mayor and said, "Mayor Leake, if you want my house tonight, you can have it."[49] Leake's success at winning the support of residents is notable, especially given that similar communities across the United States were actively mobilizing against building environmentally hazardous facilities. Towns and municipalities sought to pass ordinances to limit new facilities based on fears of pollution and possible negative health consequences.[50] Yet for the next nine months, local environmental concerns over waste incineration in Delaware County remained invisible, giving way to a ramped-up rhetoric of contested interests between a black city and its white suburbs.

As required by law, the Pennsylvania Department of Environmental Protection (PADEP) scheduled public meetings before issuing a permit to build and operate the county incinerator. The purpose of the meetings was to hear residents' concerns over any impact the incinerator might have on their community. The meetings were well attended,[51] and all the speakers objected to the county's incinerator plan, citing the county's racial and political subordination of the city with no mention of possible environmental impacts or health concerns. Vocal supporters of the mayor's plan had formed the group Concerned Citizens to Save Chester (CCSC) to mobilize and maintain the support of the city's black residents for the incinerator plan. In a May 1988 public meeting, state officials heard from a dozen CCSC members who issued complaints over a lack of self-determination, references to past and present housing and employment racial discrimination, and demands for "ownership" of the incinerator project for economic development. All the speakers objected to a PADEP operating permit based strictly on the claim that it would prevent Chester from building its own incinerator. "We are tired of handouts. We are tired of being poor folk; our city is on welfare. . . . We are tired of being walked on, sat on, spat on," one speaker concluded. PADEP officials responded that they could say nothing about Chester's incinerator project, because they had not received an application for state review and permits. They reminded the speakers that the meeting's purpose was public comment on concerns over possible traffic, noise, pollution, odors, and other impacts of the proposed county facility. None were expressed.[52]

The CCSC also targeted Chester politicians who were either lukewarm or outright opposed to the project, calling on one city councilman to resign, as "he never votes 'yes' on any positive aspect of the Chester Resource Recovery Project that would help Chester's survival."[53] Calvary Baptist Church's minister publicly leveled charges of racism at council members, claiming that Chester had been "lied to, stepped on and deceived" by county officials and that the "Ku Klux Klan is all around us." The county was determined to stop the city from building its own incinerator because its leaders did not want Chester to "earn revenues for itself because the city would then rise up out of its poverty."[54]

The city's efforts to racialize the issue mobilized many of Chester's black residents to support the incinerator, but not all. Few residents disagreed with the city's right to political self-determination, but a growing number was critical of the incinerator plan and the racial tactics used to promote it. Months after Leake's appeal to sacrifice their homes, residents had heard nothing regarding the timing, moving allowances, or property valuations from the city. Questions remained unanswered, prompting some residents of the West End to form Concerned Citizens of Flower/Pennell Streets. The group took issue with the lack of updates on the plant's financing and siting. Its members questioned why the discussion of the incinerator was cast as a city-county issue and not a local West End one, given the short- and long-term consequences for residents. Concerns voiced over the potential environmental impacts either incinerator would produce were drowned out by the representation of the city's plan as a struggle for political independence and against the white county leadership's political domination of a black city's future.[55]

By the fall of 1988 the Chester–Delaware County incinerator conflict took a decidedly more conciliatory tone. The county won approval from the state to begin construction of the Westinghouse incinerator. All that remained was for the city to sign the host agreement for the plant to be

View toward the waterfront and the Commodore Barry Bridge.

built along its waterfront. Meanwhile, the prospects for the city's project continued to deteriorate. The investigation into the $335 million bond issue left funding in limbo, and the city lost a commitment from one incinerator construction contractor and was courting another. The siting process stalled as a city council member questioned the use of a realty firm with ties to city leaders to assess the values of the homes and businesses to be cleared for the incinerator site. Most pressingly, a $1.2 million deficit in the city budget threatened to jeopardize municipal services, including police and fire protection. The county restated its standing bailout offer of $2.5 million, provided the city drop its opposition to the county's plant. In November 1988 Chester officials conceded and signed the agreement, which gave the city immediate cash to cover its deficit and millions more over the coming years. At the announcement, Leake and other officials said Chester would still pursue its own $335 million trash processing plant on the waterfront.[56]

After the city signed the host agreement, the county's plan proceeded and the Westinghouse incinerator began operation in 1991. Chester Solid Waste Associates, which owned the parcel and held a financial interest in the incinerator, proceeded to develop additional waste facilities on its site. Discussion of the city incinerator all but ceased. In 1991 the IRS invalidated the city's bond issue, officially putting an end to a project already effectively impractical. That year Leake lost the mayoral election and a Democrat became mayor of Chester for the first time in more than a century. In 1992 the city-appointed director of the trash incinerator project was convicted and imprisoned for soliciting and receiving kickbacks from contractors hired to plan and site the failed incinerator.[57] The total cost for an incinerator that was never built was $7 million.[58]

The Incinerator War That Wasn't

From its start, the city's plan to build an incinerator appeared unlikely. By 1988 both city council members and county leaders conceded that only one of the two plants could be built, as two would create too much competition for the region's trash to make either project practical. Given that the county had obtained funding and a location for its project by the time the city expressed an interest in building a competing incinerator, there was little doubt the Westinghouse incinerator would be built provided the county received the necessary state permits and the city host agreement.[59] While the city incinerator plan may appear in retrospect both a misguided effort and an exercise in incompetence, it also suggests much more about the intentional use of racial divisions in the politics of urban development.

Claims of racial subordination and limited autonomy over the city's economic development reaped considerable minority community buy in for the idea of a waste-based urban economy, as Chester residents were fixated on the ownership of an incinerator plan, not the consequences of one being built. Between 1986 and 1991 the political discourse was successfully confined to a minority community's right to build its own incinerator, not whether one should be built at all. At the start of the incinerator battle, the county plan had already secured funding and a location for its incinerator, but the plant's burn capacity, the fees to be paid to Chester, and permitting assurances for Chester Solid Waste Associates to build a multi-facility waste zone were not. These significant details, with far-reaching consequences for residents, were negotiated during the conflict between the city and the county, while public attention focused on the political drama over which of the two plans would prevail. Although county leaders actively undermined the chances of the city's incinerator being built, they never publicly dismissed the idea, indicating on repeated occasions that the city could possibly accommodate two incinerators. The terms of the extended city-county contest, the issues at hand (self-determination of a black city) and those that were not (environmental impact on the community), laid the local political groundwork for Westinghouse to build a massive incinerator and for later siting the four other waste facilities in the same waste zone with minimal community opposition.

It is not possible to conclude that the city-county incinerator war was a ruse concocted to facilitate the siting of one of the largest waste incinerator industrial parks in the United States. Yet the evidence suggests that the key terms of the deal that produced the waste zone were finalized as the supposed battle was waging. In December 1988 the Pennsylvania Crime Commission focused on the activities of Nacrelli, the Republican machine leader and former mayor of Chester (and former employer of Mayor Leake). The commission noted that Nacrelli had testified in a 1985 civil suit that he continued to maintain political control over the city's affairs, both vital and routine. In a written report the Crime Commission concluded that Nacrelli had played a significant role in mediating the incinerator dispute between the city and the county, holding several meetings with key principals, including Mayor Leake, city council members, county politicians, Westinghouse officials, and partners from RR&Z, the owners of Chester Solid Waste Associates. Nacrelli acknowledged his part in settling the dispute, referring to his role as that of a volunteer in service to the city of Chester. The Crime Commission uncovered no wrongdoing regarding Nacrelli's role in the incinerator negotiations. In its report, however, the commission concluded, "The perception that government must rely upon or call upon convicted racketeers to mediate disputes in an industry historically tainted with organized crime involvement, serves no other end but to suggest to the citizens of Chester that racketeers still decide public policy issues in the City of Chester."[60] Despite extensive testimony from key city, county, and corporate officials involved in the incinerator dispute, the commission could not conclude whether Nacrelli had clearly favored one side or the other. It appears he supported both parties during the course of the conflict as a means to broker a favorable outcome for Chester Solid Waste Associates and Westinghouse.[61]

The protracted conflict pushed racial subordination to the fore of public discourse, mobilizing salient racial tensions that lurked just below the surface of everyday life for many of Chester's black residents. Positioning the incinerator as a racial struggle resonated among many Chester residents precisely because racism, racial discrimination, and subordination were readily apparent and experienced so viscerally. The political deployment of race and racism was a cynical ploy for power that ultimately diverted community attention away from the disproportionate siting process itself.

In the Aftermath of a Parasitic Politics

Organized grassroots mobilization against Chester's waste magnet and legal charges of environmental racism eventually materialized, but only after the county's incinerator and other waste burning facilities were up and running and their impact on the surrounding communities had become apparent. The waste zone's anchor industry, the Westinghouse trash incinerator, opened in 1991. Two years later the city and county worked together to fast-track local regulatory approvals and granted exceptions and variances to land-use policies in the sixty-two-acre waste zone. Local government oversight of operations in the zone was minimal. The principal private sector stakeholder, Chester Solid Waste Associates, "retained control over every facility that has been permitted to locate in Chester, exerting direct influence over its waste-processing tenants."[62] Left out of the arrangement were the citizens of Chester, particularly the residents of the adjacent West End. Between 1991 and 1995 the Pennsylvania Department of Environmental Protection (PADEP) approved individual permits for five waste processing facilities in the fenced-off parcel, including a medical waste incinerator, a rubber tire recycling plant, and a contaminated soil recycling facility. Chester Solid Waste Associates held ownership stakes in each of the separate companies.

The border of Chester's waste zone backed up against the West End, a neighborhood of brick and masonry, flat-roofed, two-story, single-family row houses, abandoned or derelict properties, and a number of overgrown empty lots. The West End neighborhood reflected many of the economic and demographic trends that had enveloped the city proper. By 1990 Chester had lost over a third of the total manufacturing jobs present in 1950. Home values in the West End averaged $22,800, below Chester's overall average of $37,800 and far below leafy suburban Delaware County's average of $111,700. The median income in the neighborhood was $17,137, compared to $20,000 for the city and $37,000 for the entire county. In what was once a stable neighborhood housing waterfront factory workers, the number of West End households shrank to 124 home owners and 74 renters. Blacks comprised the vast majority of residents at 95 percent, whereas the proportion for the entire city in 1990 was 69 percent.[63]

Compared to other residential areas in Chester and especially suburban Delaware County (where most of the incinerator-bound trash originated), West End residents disproportionately suffered the negative impacts from the waste zone.[64] As the number of facilities permitted to operate expanded, residents dealt with a steady flow of trash trucks, odors, and noise. In their 1996 study of environmentally distressed neighborhoods, Michael Greenberg and Dona Schneider found people living directly next to mounting piles of trash awaiting incineration. Close to 50 percent of the residents living adjacent to the waste zone wanted to move out of the neighborhood. Over 40 percent of all Chester residents reported the routine nuisances of smoke and odors from adjacent plants, rats, trash on the streets, and incessant vehicle noise and traffic.[65] Another study depicted the steady stream of incinerator-bound garbage trucks through residential streets:

> Since 1991, when the incinerator opened, trucks with New York, Delaware, and Ohio license plates barreled down Thurlow Street, once a quiet residential road, often fifteen or more hours a day. The noise kept sleepy children awake until late at night, and woke them early the next morning. Their parents swept the dust that invaded their homes, and tried to get rid of the trash that flew off the heavily loaded, uncovered trucks, before it attracted the rats which arrived with the incinerator. Mothers and grandmothers watched their children as carefully as they could, to catch them before they chased a ball into the street where the trucks rattled by. Many noticed that they were coughing more, and that their kids seemed to be missing more days of school because of illness.[66]

Mounting concerns over the waste cluster's negative health impacts on West End residents prompted the U.S. Environmental Protection Agency (EPA) to conduct a risk assessment study in Chester in 1994. That year President Bill Clinton signed his Executive Order on Environmental Justice that required sixteen federal agencies to address the exposure of poor and minority communities to disproportionate levels of environmental health risks. The EPA's six-month risk assessment study examined the incidence of health problems in Chester and the West End in particular. The results released in 1995 found unacceptable cancer risks and serious noncancer risks such as kidney disease, liver disease, and respiratory problems, among residents who lived near the waste industries.[67] Chester's infant mortality rate was the highest in the state in the 1990s, and its percentage of low-weight births was nearly double that for Delaware County as a whole. The city's lung cancer mortality rate was nearly 60 percent higher than that of Delaware County. Of Chester's children, 60 percent had blood lead levels in excess of the state's threshold of safety.[68]

As the number of existing and planned facilities in the waste zone grew, residents and local environmental activists formed the grassroots organization Chester Residents Concerned for Quality Living (CRCQL). CRCQL's leader, the Chester resident Zulene Mayfield, organized petition drives and direct action protests at city hall and along the streets garbage trucks used to access the waste facilities, but to no avail. The city's and the state's responses were to permit the siting of Thermal Pure, a medical waste incinerator, and additional waste industries. The state granted Thermal Pure permission to incinerate 288 tons of infectious waste per day from Pennsylvania and surrounding states.[69] With the opening of the Thermal Pure facility in 1993, the quality of life in the West End deteriorated further. In an incident much publicized by CRCQL, a plant shutdown due to a malfunction in July 1995 left nineteen unrefrigerated truckloads of infectious medical waste on site for six days emitting a foul odor that permeated the neighborhood. In June 1995 the Pennsylvania Department of Environmental Protection (PADEP) granted another waste processing permit to Soil Remediation Systems that allowed the company to process 250,000 tons per year of petroleum-contaminated soil at the Chester waste industrial park.[70]

In May 1996 CRCQL filed a class action lawsuit against the PADEP on the basis of equal protection under Section 602 of Title VI of the 1964 Civil Rights Act.[71] The movement alleged discrimination resulting from permits the PADEP granted to five waste treatment facilities in Chester without consideration of the undue burden on nearby minority residents. Although the PADEP issued permits one facility at a time and without explicit or overt discriminatory intent, the plaintiffs claimed that the compounded polluting effects of multiple facilities operating in one place produced a cumulative negative outcome for nearby minority residents. Section 602 of Title VI requires that federal agencies adopt implementing regulations that prohibit not only intentional discrimination but also discriminatory effects. Consequently, CRCQL provided evidence of disparate impact or discriminatory effects of the agency's actions without the burden of proving intent on the part of either individuals or the agency. The lawsuit argued that when the PADEP granted a permit to the fifth waste treatment facility near the minority neighborhood, the residents suffered clear discrimination. The district court ruled in favor of the PADEP, but the Third Circuit Court of Appeals overturned that ruling in December 1997 and found that the state agency's decisions had discriminated against Chester residents.[72]

The environmental justice movement viewed the Third Circuit Court's ruling as groundbreaking, as it potentially provided environmental advocates, lawyers, and communities a less onerous legal means to fight environmentally hazardous facilities in poor and minority neighborhoods. The ruling opened the possibility of arguing that disparate impacts stemmed from structural forms of racism without demonstrating evidence of clear discriminatory intent. However, a clear victory for environmental advocates was short-lived. The U.S. Supreme Court dismissed the case in 1998 after the fifth waste industry, Soil Remediation Services, withdrew its application for a permit to operate.[73]

In addition to chasing smokestacks, Chester officials turned to another unconventional form of urban development that promised to deliver jobs and community development: housing prisoners. In the early 1990s, when incarceration levels were predicted to rise dramatically, a growing amount of federal and state dollars became available for new prison construction in primarily poorer rural towns. After intense lobbying efforts by local officials, Chester was selected as the site for a new state prison in the mid-1990s. The State Correctional Institution at Chester (or SCI-Chester) opened in 1998 as a medium security prison for male inmates with a documented history of substance abuse. It is one of only two such institutions in the United States designed to treat substance abusers in a therapeutic setting. The treatment program is a joint effort of the Pennsylvania Department of Corrections and a nonprofit addiction and mental health services corporation. State prisons are not typically built within an older city's limits. But Chester and Delaware County politicians (particularly members of the Republican Party) lobbied intensely for the Chester site, arguing that the prison would create much-needed jobs and economic spillover effects for Pennsylvania's poorest city. Chester officials were attracted by the additional revenues from federal substance abuse treatment funds that a drug rehabilitation facility would bring.

The decision to locate the prison on the waterfront adjacent to the few remaining industries (including the newer waste treatment facilities) speaks to the limited options available to Chester on the heels of decades of urban decline and a parasitic politics of extraction from the pockets of its own residents. The prison's small size blended in with an already fragmented landscape of occasional factories, empty lots, and abandoned warehouses. At the time the prison first opened, the streets across Industrial Highway were known for incidences of petty crime, small-time drug dealing, prostitution, and street gang activity. The anticipated broader, positive economic effects of penal-based development were never realized.

The Strategic Uses of Racial Stigma

Our understanding of racial and class segregation in the post–civil rights era is often depicted as de facto, the unfortunate consequence of lingering racial prejudice, the legacy of past (and now illegal) institutional discrimination, worsening economic inequality, or the lifestyles of the urban poor themselves. These lines of thinking shift our gaze away from the active forces of social exclusion and isolation. We would like to believe that active social, economic, and spatial exclusion originated in a distant past, has since been rendered illegal, and is no longer a compelling explanation for the persistence of urban poverty and exclusion. The stories in this chapter prove otherwise. Ongoing and ultimately destructive government policies and private sector interests actively reproduced and benefited from the social and spatial isolation of Chester's minority residents. The prevailing racial discourse of the inner city as dependent, threatening, self-damaging, and ultimately unsalvageable enabled this "fire sale" brand of urban politics of community pilfering, beginning with the GCM story in the late 1960s, continuing with the municipal corruption scandals of the 1970s, and ending with the invention of Chester as a waste magnet for environmentally toxic industries. Key to the city's downward trajectory is the strategic use of the racial divide to place the responsibility and blame for social and economic decline squarely on the backs of the poor black community while masking the suburban-focused white elites' profitable extraction of as much of the city's remaining value as possible. As the chapter has shown, urban decline fed on a mix of continued institutional exploitation of Chester's poor and black residents, the dissemination of discourses of fear about the black ghetto (heightened by earlier urban unrest in the city), and the clever allusion to black political leadership and participation as proof of self-governance and empowerment.

6

Welcome to the "Post-Racial" Black City

Chester today continues to be identified as a city besieged by rampant crime, poor housing conditions, joblessness, and poverty. The city hardly appears a likely candidate for private sector investment in large redevelopment projects. Yet as introduced in the opening pages of this book, private developers; investors; and local, county, and state governments have successfully completed the office complex, casino, and stadium along the waterfront, and plans are in the works to develop market-rate housing for an anticipated return of the middle class. Chester's waterfront is a testament to postindustrial urban development politics, boasting an odd and striking assortment of nondescript warehouses and small factories, an international paper products plant, a state prison, class A office space in a renovated power plant, the county's municipal trash incinerator, the Harrah's Philadelphia casino and racetrack, a cluster of renovated office spaces, and a Major League Soccer stadium. In addition, there are ambitious plans for an upscale shopping and condominium complex called Rivertown, a place-name with no historical connection to Chester whatsoever, as its developers gladly intend.

This chapter explains the most recent changes to the city's landscape by first accounting for the political economy of exclusionary development that produced—yet again—a city divided by race and class. The stark contrast between the city and the waterfront poses the question of how segregation can be reproduced and legitimized as "revitalization" well into the second decade of the twenty-first century. The answer is the employment of a race strategy embedded in the racial ideology of color blindness, as introduced in chapter 1. As this chapter explains in detail, color blindness provides ideological cover for exclusionary development, the assigning of culpability for urban decline to poor and minority residents, and the casting of residents as being in agreement or in opposition to the new Chester of middle-class consumption.

The chapter ends with a set of conclusions regarding the relevance of race strategies to the politics of urban development as spelled out in this and previous chapters. The conclusion restates the purpose of this line of inquiry into the association of race and urban change and, as importantly, what this research does not explain and why. Finally, the chapter proposes that understanding the significance of race strategies is an important step toward grassroots organizations claiming control of the narrative of urban change.

Dividing Chester

The opening of Harrah's Chester on January 22, 2007 marked an epic contrast to just a decade earlier, when the city, the state, and the local grassroots movement CRCQL were ensnared in a battle over the expansion of Chester's notorious waterfront waste zone. The waste zone earned the city the label Toxic Town USA and a place on the list "The 10 Most Corrupt Cities in America" in *George Magazine*, a now defunct political magazine.[1] Although CRCQL lost its legal battle, the movement brought sufficient attention to the issue of the city as a waste magnet. In a remarkable feat of grassroots power in a city accustomed to corrupt and ineffectual politics, the Chester City Council passed an ordinance prohibiting the future siting of new waste facilities.[2] The moratorium on new facilities gave the city a chance to redefine its future.

Chester's redeveloped waterfront marks an accomplishment for city officials, private developers, investors, and private sector partners. It also marks the triumph of market-oriented revitalization over competing visions of urban development proffered by the city's residents, neighborhood associations, and community-based organizations. Since the founding of the environmental movement CRCQL, residents have lobbied city hall to reconnect the deindustrialized waterfront to the city as part of broader community development aimed at improving social

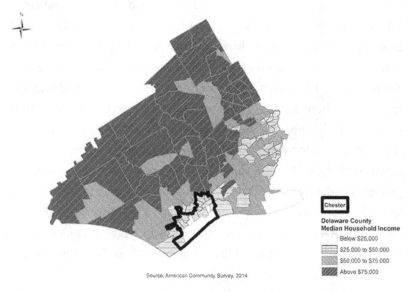

Median Household Income by Census Tract for the City of Chester and Delaware County, 2014.

and economic conditions. When the city proposed new, environmentally cleaner uses for the waterfront, residents saw an opportunity for a locally focused revitalization process that would include the construction of neighborhood facilities and recreational spaces, the revitalization of existing housing stock, improvements in public transportation, and enhanced human development such as job training programs. At the very minimum, local organizations expected an active role and a "seat at the table" of urban development decisions. Despite extensive knowledge of their own community's needs, community-based organizations and residents' advocacy groups barely participated in the entire waterfront redevelopment process.

Instead, city officials embarked on a development pathway well traveled by a number of older, former industrial cities, including nearby Camden and Baltimore, long considered impervious to private sector-driven revitalization. As a result, the city itself is once again spatially divided along race and class lines, separated by widened roads and empty lots, with the ghetto and the enclaves forming their own microcosms ranging from incarceration, bare subsistence, and legalized gambling to noxious industry, insurance underwriting, and occasional soccer games. There are few, if any, social interactions or even casual exchanges among the users of these discrete microworlds. Other than the ghetto, with its predominantly poor and black residents, the enclaves are controlled spaces intended for visitors of varied sorts: gamblers, prisoners, white-collar workers, and soccer fans. Contemporary urban development is project-based, creating islands of renewal in a sea of decay.[3] Chester itself is a much smaller and poorer city than it was fifty years ago. The current population is nearly half that of 1950. Nearly 80 percent of its residents are black, and a full third (or three times the state's average) live below the official poverty line.

The reappearance of the well-defined segregation of the small city's geography by race and class is neither unique nor unusual, given the turn in urban politics away from community development to economic development since the mid-1990s. Chester's revitalization is not intended to recreate the vision of urban renewal of the past, with its focus on addressing poor housing, unemployment, and a long list of other social and economic urban problems. The goal is neither to revive the city's past glory (for elderly, white former residents long established in the suburbs) nor to improve the current conditions for residents of the larger city. Instead, the city's urban revitalization reflects the new norm of market-oriented local economic development, publicly subsidized but directed by the private sector, with the goal of enhancing the city's competitiveness as a regional asset. This version of a more constrained and narrowly-focused urban renewal entails a revanchist reclaiming of so-called salvageable parts of poorer cities, often at the price of neglecting or further marginalizing most others. The reliance on public-private partnerships assures a return on capital investment over community development and traditional governmental mechanisms of project accountability. An extensive set of publicly financed incentives, including generous tax abatements, infrastructure development, state sanctioning of enterprise zones, and bond financing promises to deliver free-market solutions to so-called problem-plagued cities.[4]

The earliest sign of this turn to development was in 1995, when the Chester City Council created the Chester Economic Development Authority (CEDA) to be the administrative agent of redevelopment. The CEDA leveraged federal, state, and local tax abatement programs, developed proposals to secure private sector investment, and facilitated the Waterfront Overlay District, a master plan for nonindustrial development such as commercial, retail, and residential uses. Together these programs provided tax abatements, loans, and direct public investment in physical infrastructure (roads, sidewalks, parks) intended to stimulate private investment in the development of designated areas exclusively. Because these programs only apply to specifically targeted spaces, they created a locational hierarchy of economic opportunity between areas within the city. Whereas the waterfront became a specified redevelopment zone, the adjacent inner-city neighborhood was further disadvantaged by its ineligibility for state incentives to attract investment capital.

The CEDA also oversees state economic and community development funds and two key development incentive programs generated by the state and municipal governments: the Keystone Opportunity Zone (KOZ) program, which resembles enterprise zones in place in most U.S. states, and the Local Economic Revitalization Tax Assistance Act (LERTA), a state tax incentive program. KOZ is a state-initiated tax abatement and incentive program for the private redevelopment of specific zones of abandoned, unused, or underused land and buildings throughout Pennsylvania. The KOZ program provided developers of the casino and the soccer stadium with exemptions from municipal, school district, and county real estate taxes for a specified period. Corporate beneficiaries of KOZs are also exempt from taxes on earned income/ net profits, business gross receipts, sales and use, wage and net profits, realty use, and occupancy. Delaware County and the city of Chester have offered additional tax incentives to corporate relocation, development

Harrah's Philadelphia (formerly Harrah's Chester) Casino and Racetrack.

planning, and construction in KOZs. Chester implemented the state's LERTA for companies involved in the revitalization of deteriorated properties in renewal target areas. The LERTA permits private companies to defer increases in real estate taxes on the value of the improvements over ten years.

When Harrah's announced its intention to build and operate the casino in a Chester KOZ, community-based organizations and a few county and state legislators were troubled by the idea of gambling companies profiting from the tax-free zones. Yet the state law that produced KOZs only stipulated that the tax incentives be attached to the land itself and not the kinds of industries eligible for the abatement. City leaders predicted community-wide benefits from the casino, including $10 million in annual revenue for the city (roughly 20 percent of Chester's annual budget) and an anticipated spillover effect for adjacent communities. A community-based organization formed to oppose the casino's construction noted the gap between Chester's labor market and official predictions of revitalization: "There seems to be an assumption on the part of proponents of legalized gambling that the injection of new capital into the local economy, regardless of where it enters the system, will eventually trickle down to those at the bottom. We find this to be a highly dubious assumption, especially in a community where so many residents lack the training and skills to compete in the job market."[5] The CEDA was instrumental in bringing Harrah's to Chester. The agency worked with the casino industry and state officials to overcome legal restrictions and helped wage a public relations campaign to assuage concerns about gambling and the negative effects of a casino's presence on the community. The CEDA, Chester's mayor, and other city leaders portrayed Harrah's as Chester's best and last hope for breaking with its recent past and downbeat reputation as a poor, crime-ridden city. While no new restaurants, gas stations, or tourist-driven businesses have opened near the casino, Harrah's reportedly uses local vendors for some of its restaurant supplies. The company also endowed a $200,000 college scholarship for Chester students in 2008.

Just south of Harrah's is Rivertown, a multiyear, multimillion-dollar private development project that also runs along the Delaware River on former industrial land, including the former toxic dump that burned for days in 1978. The large office complex, public access pedestrian walkway along the river, and the soccer stadium are part of a larger plan that calls for the eventual development of housing, restaurants, and retail shops. In the first phase of development, investors and real estate developers purchased and renovated the former Chester Station Power Plant into an office and recreation complex called the Wharf at Rivertown. The power plant stood empty for decades and its owner, Philadelphia Electric Company, planned to demolish it until the site earned KOZ status in 1999. In October 2000 Preferred Real Estate Investments Inc. purchased the plant from Philadelphia Electric for $1 with the provision that the new owner tackle interior environmental cleanup. The cost of the cleanup of asbestos and other contaminants was $50 million.

Prior to the plant's conversion, many observers were highly skeptical of the plan to attract corporations to class A office space in Chester. First, the power plant was virtually inaccessible from roadways. The plant had been located on the waterfront for easy access to coal ships, and manufacturing plants had operated adjacent to the power plant. Empty lots replaced the warehouses and factories, and for years the electric plant stood abandoned, isolated, and inaccessible. Second, the project's developers were asking companies and their employees to put aside long-standing fears and Chester's long-lived reputation as a place overrun by crime and poverty. Working in this context of fear, risk, and considerable doubt, the Wharf's investors gained considerable concessions from city and state governments. Chester's mayor, seeing the Wharf as a showcase for the city's potential, helped Preferred secure nearly $1.1 million in public subsidies. The state provided $2.6 million in grants and loans to Preferred for infrastructure development, land reclamation, and installation of fiber optic cable. Then-senator Rick Santorum sought and won $15 million in federal assistance, mainly for a direct highway link between Rivertown and the Commodore Barry Bridge that would allow workers to bypass downtown Chester and avoid seeing or interacting with its residents.[6] A secured access road leads directly to the Wharf, and a "natural barrier" of lots made empty and laid barren by deindustrialization separates the complex from Chester's poor residential neighborhoods.

The first tenant to sign on, Synygy, was the largest single employer to locate in Chester since the city's industrial downturn in the 1960s. The firm develops and sells incentive-compensation software and services. A second tenant, AdminServer, provides back office services for life, annuity, reinsurance, and health segments of the insurance industry. AdminServer took advantage of the KOZ incentives. When the firm relocated to the Wharf, the size of its workforce grew from 26 employees operating in 6,000 square feet of office space to 225 white collar employees occupying over 40,000 square feet. A much larger property development firm, the Buccini/Pollin Group (BPG) purchased the Wharf in 2005 and immediately began to work with state and local officials to develop the remaining acreage still eligible for KOZ benefits. The BPG, private capital investors, and city, county, and state politicians, armed with promises of Pennsylvania and Delaware County funding and tax incentives, lobbied for Chester as a site for a Philadelphia Major League Soccer expansion team. In March 2008 Philadelphia was awarded the league's sixteenth franchise with its home stadium in Chester's Rivertown. Opened in 2010 and (re)named Talen Energy Stadium, the stadium is home to the Philadelphia Union team.

Like the Wharf and Harrah's, the planning, construction, and management of the soccer stadium was a joint public-private venture. State, county, and city governments partnered with Keystone Sports and Entertainment LLC, a conglomerate enterprise consisting of the BPG, private investors, and the soccer franchise. Delaware County acquired and continues to own the land that houses the 18,634-seat stadium. The commitment of private sector investment was contingent upon the county issuing a $30 million bond, $10 million from the Delaware River Port Authority for waterfront improvements, and $25 million in state aid (with a promise of additional funds for future mixed-use development). The second phase of the development calls for a mix of townhomes, apartments, retail and office space, and a convention center. The state's transportation agency constructed exit ramps from Route 322/Interstate 95, allowing motorists direct access to the stadium without driving through Chester's poorest neighborhoods.

Together, local development authorities and tax abatement programs comprise an innovative and powerful set of governance mechanisms that directly facilitate fragmented and exclusionary forms of urban redevelopment. In Chester the use of KOZ-designated subsidies means development is project and site specific. Chester's KOZs favor a doughnut-shaped pattern of development in which newer, upscale sites ring the poorest residential neighborhoods and the defunct central business district. The zones are also not contiguous, leading to fragmented redevelopment. Newer developments, then, are disconnected from the urban core, allowing, if not encouraging, developers to define their projects as distinct from the city proper.

Inventing a Post-Racial Black City

City leaders and developers contend that the casino, the soccer stadium, and the proposed residential and entertainment complex will eventually spur development in the surrounding city (across the dividing line of Route 291). Even prior to the completion of the soccer stadium, the editors of the *Delaware County Daily Times* pointed out that "development along the riverfront will only have true meaning for the city if it crosses Route 291 and spreads to all neighborhoods in the city."[7] However, the type of project-specific, highly subsidized development Chester has embarked on makes a spillover effect improbable. There are no development incentives for small shopkeepers or owners of small parcels surrounding Harrah's or Rivertown. Harrah's opened its doors ten years ago, and the Philadelphia Union's first home game was June 27, 2010. There is little evidence of the much-promised economic spillover from either redevelopment project. Amid dilapidated row houses, empty storefronts, and abandoned lots, a handful of small corner groceries, an auto shop, a pharmacy, and a number of bars, taverns, and liquor stores struggle to remain in business. After years of waiting for the benefits of redevelopment to materialize, many locals are skeptical. In a letter to the local newspaper, for example, a council member asserted: "Let's be real. The new [Route] 291 has become a dividing line, with rich people on one side and the not so rich on the other. I don't see people kicking down doors for a soccer stadium in Chester. I am not saying we should block it, but how about a real supermarket first?"[8]

Chester residents have lived without a full-fledged, large grocery store since the West End Food Center closed in August 2001. For many residents, including the elderly, the disabled, and those without private means of transport, shopping for food and groceries involves a lengthy bus trip to supermarkets in surrounding towns and suburbs. After the opening of Harrah's casino in 2007, a handful of residents and representatives of neighborhood block associations questioned why the city's redevelopment did not include plans to attract a new supermarket. But

Chester's central business district.

the opening of a major supermarket does not meet the current standard of local economic development. While local development officials agree that a supermarket in the city is a priority for residents, neither the government nor the private sector are willing to invest. Residents must wait for more favorable free-market forces to prevail.[9]

The supermarket issue speaks to the difficulties of meeting basic living needs for the majority of the city's poor and black residents. A casino and racetrack and a soccer stadium qualify as viable local economic development projects, but a supermarket does not. But Chester's black residents have not simply been left behind by the new developments along the waterfront. The employment of the latest race strategy, color blindness or race neutrality, has several implications for Chester's poor minority residents. First, the ideology and rhetoric of color blindness substitute an emphasis on individual culpability for institutional racism as the cause of urban social problems. Color-blind racial ideology

strips contemporary urban racial inequalities of their historical rooted-
ness and structural causes, leaving behind only the cultural characteristics of affected individuals themselves as the focus of explanation.[10]
Unemployment, weak social ties, high crime rates, and a host of other
social problems are not manifestations of structural inequalities but are
"primarily attributable to blacks themselves, to their lack of work ethic
or impulse control, their irresponsibility, and other internally control-
lable factors."[11]

Subsequently, social policies and other forms of governmental
intervention—especially urban renewal—are of limited use in solving
individualized problems (as the supermarket issue suggests). In the redefining of race from a social category to that of individual identity (or
even preference), a color-blind ideology rejects collective, public sphere
solutions to difficulties best addressed by individuals themselves or locally based community organizations. The elimination of race as a truly
collective or social category and the subsequent individualizing of social
problems dovetails with continued calls for the further elimination of
a range of social welfare policies. The color-blind formulation of race
as cultural identity anchors causes and solutions to urban problems in
the private, not the social, sphere.[12] As a race strategy employed to legitimize current urban development, color blindness relieves local, state,
and federal governments from responsibilities to the minority poor and
directs them to assisting and subsidizing the private sector (under the
guise of revitalization). The declining significance of race masks the
retraction of government social policies and the turn toward enabling
the "free market"—which, as indicated in the last chapter, was largely
responsible for urban decline in the first place.

Third, color blindness negates the legitimacy of collective action
among black residents at the neighborhood or community level. In his
critique of color-blind racism, Henry Giroux maintains that "inherent
in the logic of color blindness is the central assumption that race has no
valence as a marker of identity or power when factored into the social
vocabulary of everyday life and the capacity for exercising individual

and social agency."[13] Stripped of its potential for political and potentially subversive mobilization, race no longer serves as a "basis for citizen-based action" on matters of urban or economic development.[14] Chester's political leaders recognize the importance of community-based organizations as providers of civic and social welfare services. But community organizations do not qualify as stakeholders in urban development; the progrowth orientation of urban politics extols the private sector's leadership in planning, financing, and deal brokering. In the zeal to redevelop the waterfront, therefore, the meaningful efforts of residents to improve their city do not conform to the economic development mandate of making Chester a destination for outsiders.[15]

Finally, the race strategy of color blindness allows for the political view of the city's residents as individuals who either fit in or comply with the lofty goals of redevelopment or do not. For city officials, county politicians, and developers, the revived Chester is a "small riverfront community" with unrivaled transportation access to Philadelphia and its exurbs. Promotional brochures, websites, and other materials make the case that the waterfront development will enhance Chester's civic identity and its racial and cultural diversity. Promotional materials depict a polyglot of individuals of both genders and of diverse ages, apparent class statuses, races, and ethnicities interacting and enjoying the new Chester in striking contrast to the city's recent past (or its present reality for the majority of residents). Indeed, developers and city officials remain anxious that elements of the "old Chester" may resurface and upset the cozy narrative of a city on a clear path toward renewal.

Their fears came to the fore in the summer of 2010. In the week prior to the official opening of the new soccer stadium, four Chester residents were shot and killed. To the dismay of public officials, waterfront development officials, and corporate sponsors, Chester's "murder capital" reputation was revived just as another linchpin in the city's revival was to be unveiled. The mayor imposed a nighttime curfew in five high-crime neighborhoods. Dubbed "martial law" by the local and national press, the mayor's action was intended to reassure the media, visitors, and soccer fans that the violence was not rampant but concentrated in specific, "problem" neighborhoods not near the waterfront. Some residents welcomed the mayor's crackdown on violent crime regardless of the underlying rationale for doing so. Many others viewed the curfew as an eye-catching but unsustainable fix for a complex social problem. Most understood that the curfew was for the benefit of the much-coveted outsiders and not the city's residents. Opening day was problem free, but the phalanx of police officers lining the road to the soccer stadium assured everyone that the old Chester would not get in the way of its own renewal.[16]

Under the progrowth politics of development, claims of enhanced diversity refer specifically to the return of predominantly white, middle-class suburbanites as visitors and eventually as residents. Enhancing diversity by no way means the inclusion of the city's disadvantaged minority population writ large. The new Chester is inclusive to the extent that everyone is welcome as a potential worker or preferably, consumer. Some residents are employed in low-paying, part-time positions as maintenance staff, cooks, and helpers in restaurants, valet attendants, and some security positions in the casino and the soccer stadium facilities. In the case of the casino, most of the higher paying positions, which require extensive criminal and credit background checks in addition to casino experience, have been filled by persons relocated from other Harrah's properties. For most residents, however, the waterfront offers few reasons to visit.

The progrowth politics of current development also questions the rightful claims of poor and minority residents as stakeholders in their city's future. Residents have a shrinking right to the city unless they participate as responsible consumers or at minimum conduct themselves in a manner conducive to consumption. In his work on the larger social consequences of consumerism, Zygmunt Bauman argues that the poor, as "collateral casualties of consumerism," have "no merits to relieve, let alone redeem, their vices. They have nothing to offer in exchange for the taxpayers' outlays. Money transferred to them is a bad investment, unlikely to be repaid, let alone to bring profit. . . . Unneeded, unwanted, forsaken—where is their place? The briefest of answers is: out of sight."[17] All told, the employment of the race strategy of color blindness facilitates and legitimizes exclusionary urban development as defensible, desirable, and essential to the improvement of Chester. The "post-racial" Chester turns its back on its racialized past and instead aspires toward a fully entrepreneurial city in which the energies and resources of both the public and the private sectors are directed at attracting capital investment and achieving the universal good of economic development. The race strategy of color blindness renders exclusionary redevelopment possible and even unproblematic in a city as impoverished as Chester.

Employing Race in Urban Development: From Strategy to Tactic

This study of Chester has provided concrete accounts of how the local politics of urban development is consistently and strategically anchored in the ideologies and rhetoric of race. Race does not simply provide an ideological context or backdrop in which episodes of urban development unfold. Rather, the association of race with the local politics of development is much more intimate and visceral. As the stories recounted in this book show, the association is systematic and intentional; it is strategic. Exploring race as systematically (but not uniformly) employed over the course of a city's history reveals that race is immensely practical to the politics of urban development. The incidents in which race strategies are employed should not be viewed as aberrations or the results of rogue individuals harboring and acting on racist attitudes. Race strategies are repeatedly shown to be practical and effective in the routine expression of institutional power over the course of urban development—in economic investment and disinvestment in the built environment, in the siting of environmentally harmful industries, or in the production of destinations in urban enterprise zones, to name but a few.

Race has held a special significance for urban change in Chester ever since the Great Migration of blacks to the city in the early decades of the twentieth century. But demographics tell only part of the story, as race and racism quickly became normalized in the local politics of place and urban and suburban development. The political embrace of race strategies provided the legitimacy and justification for institutional practices such as mortgage lending that excluded minorities and also motivations for individuals and entire communities to behave in a racist and at times violent manner, such as keeping black families out of their suburban homes. The resistance of Chester's political elites to enforcing federal standards beginning in the late 1960s allowed political provincialism to prevail uninterrupted, and race consistently remained front and center in the spatial politics well into the 2000s. The employment of race strategies influenced collective preferences regarding where (and where not) to live, work, and socialize, further socially and spatially isolating those already experiencing exclusion. In turn, local power holders reaped the benefits of systematically draining resources from a city they helped vilify. Chester's black citizens could not look to their local government to act impartially on their behalf but instead watched it reproduce and promote broader racist interests embedded in urban and regional development.

Over the course of the past century, the strategic employment of race in local politics has vilified black neighborhoods, the ghetto, and eventually the entire city as a place of ongoing desperation and rampant social pathologies. As the events recounted here attest, the vilification of black spaces proved strategic and valuable to the political economy of spatial change. The point of this book is not to test or contest the veracity of such demonizing representations and discourses—to do so would devolve into a tricky discussion of the moral standing of social behaviors, potentially casting inner-city residents as hapless victims, as dysfunctional perpetrators, or as upstanding citizens in the face of overwhelming social and economic challenges.[18] It is more than likely that all these and countless other "types" of individuals live in Chester, and we would expect the same in suburban Delaware County or anywhere else, for that matter. The systematic and strategic functionality of racial claims is the focus of this book, not the accuracy of the claims themselves.

We can conclude with confidence that the chasm between how the ghetto is represented and how inner-city life is actually experienced is vast. It would be a grave error to assume that the majority of the meaningful everyday practices of poor black residents are guided by racial discourses and related ideologies that serve the politics of urban development. Indeed, we can expect the reverse—even the most mundane and routine interactions and ways of being may serve as everyday practices of resistance to power and exclusion. Perhaps most importantly, an effort to "test" the depictions of the ghetto and black experience would invariably lead to a reification of the inner city as a cohesive space populated by one or more social types. Chester may or may not be home to the stereotypical inner-city bad actors, the ennobled good citizens who combat them, and many others who fit somewhere in between. To take on the veracity of racially coded discourses would end up perversely validating the very vocabulary of black life that the race strategies discussed in this book sought to reproduce. To do so would contribute very little to an understanding of how race strategies function as a powerful force in the political economy of urban development.

It is important to note the political relevance of challenging race strategies "from below," as the employment of race in urban politics "crowds out" the efforts and voices of residents seeking to better the place they call home. This was abundantly clear in the civil rights actions of 1963 and 1964, when thousands of Chester's residents protested against the overt racial discrimination that prevailed in their schools, housing, and public spaces. Direct action, through boycotts, sit-ins, and mass demonstrations brought about important changes to the racial status quo in the short term. However, the possibilities for durable social change were quickly smothered by a cynical form of politics that robbed a community's righteous anger to serve its own ends. In short, race strategies routinely result in the erasure of an organic, community politics, as the city and its inhabitants are routinely cast as (stereo)types that prove useful to the pursuit of a development agenda. Because the employment of racial rhetoric and discourses by political leaders, developers, and other private stakeholders is, as this book has argued, intentional, we should expect effective forms of grassroots resistance.

This book has maintained that race is deployed as part of a governance that legitimizes inequalities and injustices in Chester and cities like it. At no point in Chester's history were the voices of local black residents absent or completely silenced. But all too frequently they were not heard above the din of those in political and economic control who manipulated race for political and economic gain. From a collective action standpoint, the preceding chapters point to the need for local communities to forcibly promote their own narratives of urban change. The task is to engage with, understand, and support the emergence of a counterpolitics in which local communities themselves employ race as a tactic against exclusionary forms of urban development. Gaining control of the symbolic politics of defining the direction of urban change may seem superficial in comparison to the very tangible resource demands of community organizing. But the chapters in this book suggest the importance of controlling the narrative that influences the course of urban development. If urban transformation is to be inclusive, meaningful, and truly consensual, then local communities are compelled to fight those in power for the ability to define the message of renewal—of which race is front and center. Sustained efforts to gain control of the narrative of development rest on the local consensual determination of social problems and needs. This involves a grassroots politics of defining and broadcasting a community's version of urban development. If the narrative of urban change is defined externally, similar patterns of inequality and exclusion are bound to be repeated. A grassroots politics that employs a tactic of race as reflective of a community's realities and aspirations is a counterpolitics to the entrepreneurial turn in urban development, where the significance of race (and, more importantly, racism) is denied. In such an environment the possibilities for building cities that contest rather than perpetuate the marginalization of its existing communities are enhanced.

NOTES

CHAPTER 1. RACE STRATEGIES AND THE POLITICS OF URBAN DEVELOPMENT

1 Neighborhood Scout, "Neighborhood Scout's Most Dangerous Cities—2015," www.neighborhoodscout.com. Accessed March 1, 2015.

2 Erik Eckholm, "A City Celebrates a Brand New Stadium, but Not after 9 P.M. in Some Quarters," *New York Times*, June 27, 2010.

3 Color blindness or race neutrality conceives of race exclusively as an individual identity construct and not as a category produced systematically and historically through exploitation and discrimination. Ideologically, it denies a group's position within a racial hierarchy that influences access to resources and delineates social outcomes and replaces it with a depoliticized identity unrelated to systemic inequalities. This formal rejection of systemic racism suggests that race—as a social category and a marker of structured disadvantage—is no longer a basis for individual or group social or political standing. Contemporary charges of unresolved racism and racial inequalities, which tend to call for intervention on the part of states and social institutions, are eviscerated. See Eduardo Bonilla-Silva, *Racism without Racists: Color-Blind Racism and the Persistence of Racial Inequality in the United States* (Lanham, Md.: Rowman and Littlefield, 2009); Eduardo Bonilla-Silva and David Dietrich, "The Sweet Enchantment of Color-Blind Racism in Obamerica," *Annals of the American Academy of Political and Social Science* 634, no. 1 (2011): 190–206; Michael K. Brown, Martin Carnoy, Elliot Currie, Troy Duster, David B. Oppenheimer, Marjorie M. Shultz, and David Wellman, *Whitewashing Race: The Myth of a Color-Blind Society* (Berkeley: University of California Press, 2003); David J. Roberts and Minnele Mahtani, "Neoliberalizing Race, Racing Neoliberalism: Placing 'Race' in Neoliberal Discourses," *Antipode* 42, no. 2 (2010): 248–257; Henry A. Giroux, *Against the Terror of Neoliberalism: Politics beyond the Age of Greed* (London: Paradigm, 2008); Lisa Duggan, *The Twilight of Equality? Neoliberalism, Cultural Politics, and the Attack on Democracy* (Boston: Beacon, 2003); Christopher Mele, "Neoliberalism, Race, and the Redefining of Urban Redevelopment," *International Journal of Urban and Regional Research* 37, no. 2 (2013): 598–617. Color-blind racial ideology strips the realities of contemporary urban poverty from their historical antecedents and structural causes, leaving nothing behind but the cultural characteristics of the affected individuals

themselves as the focus of explanation. See Kenneth J. Neubeck and Noel A. Cazenave, *Welfare Racism: Playing the Race Card against America's Poor* (New York: Routledge, 2001).

4 Bonilla-Silva, *Racism without Racists*, 2. See also David Theo Goldberg, *The Threat of Race: Reflections on Racial Neoliberalism* (Malden, Mass.: Wiley-Blackwell, 2009).

5 I use the terms "rhetoric," "representations," and "discourses" interchangeably to refer to various combinations of language, narratives, professional terminologies, and popular images that circulate in news articles, fiction, policies, and other forms of public documents and privilege and affirm ideological frameworks regarding race and racism. Discourses and representations endorsed by those with power and authority influence how "race" is talked and written about, experienced, and understood and thereby dominate privileged meanings while excluding others. See Martin Reisigl and Ruth Wodak, *Discourse and Discrimination: Rhetorics of Racism and Antisemitism* (New York: Routledge, 2005).

6 The debate on whether and how much segregation has declined is largely a methodological one pertaining to questions of geographic scale and definitions of racial categories. See Robert Adelman and Christopher Mele, eds., *Race, Space, and Exclusion: Segregation and Beyond in Metropolitan America* (New York: Routledge, 2015); Nancy A. Denton, "Interpreting U.S. Segregation Trends: Two Perspectives," *City and Community* 12, no. 2 (2013): 156–159; Edward Glaeser and Jacob Vigdor, *The End of the Segregated Century: Racial Separation in America's Neighborhoods, 1890–2010*, Civic Report no. 66 (New York: Manhattan Institute, 2012); Richard Alba and Steven Romalewski, *The End of Segregation? Hardly* (New York: CUNY Graduate Center, Center for Urban Research, 2012); John Logan and Brian Stults, *The Persistence of Segregation in the Metropolis: New Findings from the 2010 Census*, census brief prepared for Project US2010 (Providence, R.I.: US 2010, 2011).

7 Georg Simmel, "The Sociology of Space," in David Frisby and Mike Featherstone, eds., *Simmel on Culture* (London: Sage, 1997 [1903]), 143.

8 *New York Times*, "Riots Mar Peace in Chester, PA," April 26, 1964.

9 Eduardo Bonilla-Silva, "More Than Prejudice: Restatement, Reflections, and New Directions in Critical Race Theory," *Sociology of Race and Ethnicity* 1, no. 1 (2015): 82.

10 See Arnold Hirsch, "With or without Jim Crow: Black Residential Segregation in the United States," in Arnold Hirsch and Raymond H. Mohl, eds., *Urban Policy in Twentieth-Century America* (New Brunswick, N.J.: Rutgers University Press, 1993), 65–99; Gregory Squires, *Capital and Communities in Black and White: The Intersections of Race, Class, and Uneven Development* (Albany: SUNY Press, 1994); Thomas J. Sugrue, *The Origins of the Urban Crisis: Race and Inequality in Postwar Detroit* (Princeton: Princeton University Press, 1996). Also see relevant sections in

Joe R. Feagin and Robert Parker, *Building American Cities: The Urban Real Estate Game*, 2nd ed. (Englewood Cliffs, N.J.: Prentice Hall, 1990).

11 Kevin Fox Gotham, *Race, Real Estate, and Uneven Development: The Kansas City Experience, 1900–2000* (Albany: SUNY Press, 2002).

CHAPTER 2. THE RACIAL DIVIDE IN THE MAKING OF CHESTER

1 John Ihlder, "How the War Came to Chester: A Study of the War's Effect upon Living Conditions," study prepared for the Philadelphia Housing Authority, MS, Delaware County Historical Society, Chester, Pa., 1918, 243. Chester was a stop for trains along the Pennsylvania Railroad's New York-Washington route up to the late 1960s. Since 1976 Amtrak trains running along the Northeast Corridor have no longer stopped in Chester.

2 Elliott M. Rudwick, *Race Riot in East St. Louis, July 2, 1917* (Carbondale: Southern Illinois University Press, 1964), 3.

3 John Morrison McLarnon III, "Ruling Suburbia: A Biography of the McClure Machine of Delaware County, Pennsylvania," Ph.D. diss., University of Delaware (1997), 17.

4 Ibid., 46–49.

5 Ibid., 42.

6 Richard Harris, *Politics and Prejudice: Small-Town Blacks Battle a Corrupt System* (Media, Pa.: Changing Outlook, 2008), 20–48.

7 Martin Kilson, "Political Change in the Negro Ghetto, 1900–1940s," in Nathan Irvin Huggins, Martin Kilson, Daniel M. Fox, and John Morton Blum, eds., *Key Issues in the Afro-American Experience* (New York: Harcourt Brace Jovanovich, 1971), 167–192.

8 Ihlder, "How the War Came to Chester," 244. The population increase was short-lived, as the total population dropped to 58,000 in 1920.

9 McLarnon, "Ruling Suburbia," 82.

10 Ibid., 82–83; Ihlder, "How the War Came to Chester," 244.

11 Ihlder, "How the War Came to Chester," 244.

12 McLarnon, "Ruling Suburbia," 62.

13 Daniel R. Fusfeld and Timothy Bates, *The Political Economy of the Urban Ghetto* (Carbondale: Southern Illinois University Press, 1984), 17–23.

14 Ihlder, "How the War Came to Chester," 243.

15 McLarnon, "Ruling Suburbia," 122.

16 Ibid.

17 Jennifer Leigh-Shatto Craighead, "Quest for Freedom: The Chester Race Riot of 1917," MS, Millersville University, 1990. See also newspaper accounts of the riots in the Race Riots file at the Delaware County Historical Society, Chester, Pa., including *Chester Times*, July 26–31, 1917; *Philadelphia North American*, July 26–31, 1917; *Philadelphia Evening Bulletin*, July 26–31, 1917; *New York Times*, July 26–27, 29, 1917.

18 *Philadelphia North American*, "Chester Riots," August 4, 1917, cited in McLarnon, "Ruling Suburbia," 128–129.

19 McLarnon, "Ruling Suburbia," 129–132.

20 Harris, *Politics and Prejudice*, 30.

21 Ibid., 31.

22 McLarnon, "Ruling Suburbia," 292–293.

23 Ibid., 298.

24 Ibid., 300–330.

25 National Labor Review Board, "In the Matter of Sun Shipbuilding and Dry Dock Co. and Industrial Union of Marine and Shipbuilding Workers of America," 38, no. 63 (January 15, 1942): 239–240. Hereafter cited as NLRB.

26 McLarnon, "Ruling Suburbia," 366; John Morrison McLarnon III, "Pie in the Sky vs. Meat and Potatoes: The Case of Sun Ship's Yard No. 4," *Journal of American Studies* 34, no. 1 (2000): 67–88.

27 NLRB, "In the Matter of Sun Shipbuilding and Dry Dock Co. and Industrial Union of Marine and Shipbuilding Workers of America," 244.

28 Ibid., 264.

29 NLRB, "In the Matter of Sun Shipbuilding and Dry Dock Company and Pattern Makers' League of America," 14, no. 23 (August 7, 1939): 295.

30 McLarnon, "Ruling Suburbia," 369.

31 NLRB, "In the Matter of Sun Shipbuilding and Dry Dock Co. and Industrial Union of Marine and Shipbuilding Workers of America," 236.

32 Ibid., 234; *National Labor Relations Board v. Sun Shipbuilding and Dry Dock Co.* (1943); *Shipyard Worker*, October 9, 1942; *Shipyard Worker*, April 2, 1943.

33 National Urban League, *Summary and Recommendations of the Review of the Economic and Cultural Problems of the Negro Population of Chester, Media, and Darby Township: Survey of Race Relations and Negro Living Conditions in Delaware County*, MS, Delaware County Historical Society, Chester, Pa., April–May 1946.

34 Herbert R. Northrup, "Negroes in a War Industry: The Case of Shipbuilding," *Journal of Business of the University of Chicago* 16, no. 3 (July 1943): 160–172.

35 *Chester Times*, "Urban League Report: Employment," April 11, 1947.

36 *Chester Times*, "35-Year-Old Sun Shipyard Reached Peak in World War II with 350 Vessels Built," n.d., 1951.

37 Herbert R. Northrup, *Organized Labor and the Negro* (New York: Harper, 1944), 220–221; *National Labor Relations Board v. Sun Shipbuilding and Dry Dock Co.*, 1371–1395.

38 Northrup, *Organized Labor*, 221.

39 Harris, *Politics and Prejudice*, 67.

40 Northrup, *Organized Labor*, 222.

41 Ibid., 221–223.

42 Ibid., 223–224.

43 Fusfeld and Bates, *The Political Economy*, 18.

44 *Chester Times*, "Urban League Report: Employment"; J. J. Joseph, "The Mobilization of Man-Power," *Science and Society* 7, no. 1 (Winter 1943): 2–13.

CHAPTER 3. HOW TO MAKE A GHETTO

  1 *Chester Times*, "Urban League Report on Negro Conditions Bared," April 9, 1947; *Chester Times*, "Urban League Report Seen as Significant by Dr. Aubrey," April 10, 1947.

  2 National Urban League, *Summary and Recommendations*.

  3 *Chester Times*, "Urban League Report: Housing," April 12, 1947; National Urban League, *Summary and Recommendations*.

  4 *New York Times*, "War Houses at Auction," March 12, 1922.

  5 McLarnon, "Ruling Suburbia," 531–532.

  6 Papers of the NAACP, Part 5, *The Campaign against Residential Segregation, 1914–1955*.

  7 Ibid.

  8 McLarnon, "Ruling Suburbia," 532.

  9 John Morrison McLarnon III, "'Old Scratchhead' Reconsidered: George Raymond and Civil Rights in Chester, Pennsylvania," *Pennsylvania History* 69, no. 3 (1999): 297–341.

10 McLarnon, "Pie in the Sky," 68.

11 Ibid.

12 McLarnon, "Ruling Suburbia," 528.

13 Ibid., 529.

14 King began his studies at Crozer Theological Seminary on September 14, 1948 and graduated on May 8, 1951 with a bachelor of divinity degree. Barbour often invited King to his home for dinner and conversation. King lived at Crozer and spent much of his free time on its campus. But when he did venture out in Chester, he experienced discrimination in restaurants and other public spaces. See Clayborne Carson, "Martin Luther King Jr.: The Crozer Seminary Years," *Journal of Blacks in Higher Education* 16 (Summer 1997): 123–128.

15 *Chester Times*, "Urban League Report: Housing."

16 Not until the passage of the Fair Housing Act in 1968 were restrictive covenants deemed invalid and their practice illegal (as opposed to simply unenforceable, as indicated in the 1948 Supreme Court ruling). See Kevin Fox Gotham, "Urban Space, Restrictive Covenants, and the Origins of Racial Residential Segregation in a U.S. City, 1900–1950," *International Journal of Urban and Regional Research* 24, no. 3 (2000): 616–633.

17 *Chester Times*, "Wissler Criticizes PHA Reporting," November 6, 1956.

18 McLarnon, "Ruling Suburbia," 355.

19 Ibid., 531.

20 *Chester Times*, "Wholesale Evictions of High Income Families Planned in Home Projects," May 15, 1947.

21 McLarnon, "Ruling Suburbia," 532.

22 *Chester Times*, "Negro Housing Still Critical Report Shows," March 19, 1948; McLarnon, "Ruling Suburbia," 532.

23 *Chester Times*, "Wissler Resigns as Head of CHA, Cites Meddling," September 25, 1957.

24 *Chester Times*, "CHA Desegregation Policy Given Court Confirmation," March 8, 1957.

25 *Chester Times*, "Wissler Resigns."

26 *Chester Times*, "Housing Authority Moves to Expand Integration Plan," February 5, 1957.

27 McLarnon, "Ruling Suburbia," 533.

28 *Delaware County Daily Times*, "CHA Ordered to Desegregate Public Housing," May 5, 1972.

29 *Chester Times*, "Chester's Suburbs Have Grown Up Along with the City," September 7, 1951.

30 Chester City Planning Commission, *Comprehensive Plan*, MS, Delaware County Historical Society, Chester, Pa., 1965, 3.

31 McLarnon, "Ruling Suburbia," 425.

32 Health and Welfare Council of Delaware, Montgomery, and Philadelphia Counties, *The City of Chester: Its Population and Housing* (n.p.: n.p., 1963).

33 Papers of the NAACP, Part 27, *Selected Branch Files, 1956–1965*, Series B, *The Northeast*.

34 Brent Staples, *Parallel Time: Growing Up in Black and White* (New York: Pantheon, 1994), 61.

35 Ibid., 73.

36 McLarnon, "Ruling Suburbia," 171.

37 Ibid., 437.

38 Ibid., 443.

39 Ibid., 173.

40 G. Edward Janosik, "Suburban Balance of Power," *American Quarterly* 17, no. 2 (1955): 133–134.

41 McLarnon, "Ruling Suburbia," 425.

42 Ibid., 173.

43 Ibid., 431–432.

44 Quoted in Sue Carroll Edwards, "Housing Desegregation in a Small Town," *Friends Journal*, February 15, 2012, www.friendsjournal.org.

45 Stanley Keith Arnold, *Building the Beloved Community: Philadelphia's Interracial Civil Rights Organizations and Race Relations, 1930–1970* (Jackson: University Press of Mississippi, 2014).

46 *Chester Times*, "1st Negro Home in Rutledge Burns, 2-Pronged Arson Probe Launched," May 26, 1958; *Chester Times*, "Police Press Search for Rutledge Clues," May 27, 1958; *Chester Times*, "Arson Probe Upsets Rutledge, but Nobody Points a

Finger," May 28, 1958; *Chester Times*, "Way Cleared to Rebuild Burned Home Negro Owns," March 5, 1959; *Chester Times*, "Raymond Rebuilding Burned Rutledge Home," March 6, 1959.

47 Glenn A. McCurdy, "The Folcroft Incident," *Negro Digest* 14, no. 2 (December 1964): 88.

48 Ibid., 91.

49 Ibid., 93–94.

50 *Delaware County Daily Times*, "Crowd Jeers Negroes," August 29, 1963; *Delaware County Daily Times*, "Race Crisis Boils in Folcroft," August 30, 1963; *Delaware County Daily Times*, "Police Enforce Racial Peace," August 31, 1963; *Delaware County Daily Times*, "Folcroft Action Mapped," September 13, 1963.

51 McCurdy, "The Folcroft Incident," 95. See also *Philadelphia Inquirer*, "Folcroft Home Fired by 'Molotov Cocktail' Despite Police Cordon," August 30, 1963; *Philadelphia Inquirer*, "Police Battle 1500 in Folcroft as Negroes Huddle in Cellar," August 31, 1963; *Philadelphia Inquirer*, "Uneasy Folcroft Is Placed under Tight Police Guard," September 1, 1963.

52 McCurdy, "The Folcroft Incident," 95.

53 Ibid.

54 *Philadelphia Bulletin*, "Bakers Put Home Up for Sale, Will Move from Folcroft," April 1, 1966.

55 See a similar argument in William N. Piggot, "The Geography of Exclusion: Race and Suburbanization in Postwar Philadelphia," MA thesis, Ohio State University (2002), 45–46.

56 McLarnon, "Ruling Suburbia," 540.

57 Chester City Planning Commission, *Comprehensive Plan*, MS, Delaware County Historical Society, Chester, Pa., 1964; Chester City Planning Commission, *Comprehensive Plan*, 1965.

CHAPTER 4. THE BIRMINGHAM OF THE NORTH

1 *New York Times*, "Riots Mar Peace."

2 Chester City Planning Commission, *Comprehensive Plan*, 1964, 10–14.

3 Ibid.

4 Ibid.; Chester City Planning Commission, *Comprehensive Plan*, 1965; McLarnon, "Ruling Suburbia," 545–546.

5 Health and Welfare Council, *The City of Chester*, 12.

6 Harris, *Politics and Prejudice*, 50–51.

7 *Chester NAACP Scrapbook 1963–1964*, courtesy of the family of George Raymond. Wolfgram Library, Widener University.

8 Papers of the NAACP, Part 23, *Legal Department Case Files, 1957–1965*, Series B, *The Northeast*.

9 Governor's Commission Investigating Recent Events in Chester, Pennsylvania, *Report of the Commission Appointed by the Governor to Investigate Charges of*

Excessive Use of Force by Police in Chester, Pennsylvania (Harrisburg, Pa.: n.p., 1964), 10–11.

10 Papers of the NAACP, Part 23.

11 Ibid.

12 Ibid., *Chester School District v. Chester Branch of the NAACP and CFFN*.

13 Papers of the NAACP, Part 25, Series B, *1956–1965*.

14 Paul Bender, *Police Brutality in Chester, Pennsylvania, March–April 1964: Report Prepared for the Greater Philadelphia Branch of the American Civil Liberties Union*, June 30, 1964, 3.

15 Danny Pope, Alain Jehlen, Evan Metcalf, and Cathy Wilkerson, "Chester, PA: A Case Study in Community Organization," Students for a Democratic Society working paper, 1964, 2.

16 In March 1963 Branche and eight others were arrested for attempting to block the eviction of a thirty-seven-year-old tenant from the Ruth L. Bennett Homes public housing project. The CHA claimed that the single-mother tenant had violated the Richmond Agreement, a 1957 ruling barring single mothers from having additional children out of wedlock while residing in public housing. As CHA workers emptied the apartment of its furniture and other contents, Branche and his fellow demonstrators formed a human chain to block the moving van. Shortly after they were arrested and charged with misdemeanor obstruction, the NAACP posted bail for them. Much to the chagrin of NAACP leaders, the *Delaware County Daily Times* identified Branche as "the local executive director of the NAACP": *Delaware County Daily Times*, "Chester NAACP Official Is Arrested," March 2, 1963. Five days after his arrest, Branche organized a group of fifteen protesters, including some local suburban college students, to picket the CHA for its policies that supervised the morality of its minority tenants. See *Delaware County Daily Times*, "Pickets Walk, Stand, Sit in Eviction Protest," March 7, 1963; Papers of the NAACP, Part 1, *Meetings of the Board of Directors, Records of Annual Conferences, Major Speeches, and Special Reports, 1909–1950*, Supplement to Part 1, *Minutes of the Board of Directors, Secretary's Reports, Records of Annual Conventions, and Annual Business Meetings, 1961–1965, 1963*.

17 Bender, *Police Brutality in Chester*, 3; *Delaware County Daily Times*, "Merchants Threatened by NAACP," April 19, 1963.

18 *Delaware County Daily Times*, "NAACP Offered Outside Aid," June 15, 1963.

19 *Delaware County Daily Times*, "Human Relations Meeting Called Off," July 18, 1963.

20 *Delaware County Daily Times*, "Will Schism Shatter Chester NAACP?" September 20, 1963.

21 Bender, *Police Brutality in Chester*, 4; Paul Lyons, *The People of This Generation: The Rise and Fall of the New Left in Philadelphia* (Philadelphia: University of Pennsylvania Press, 2003).

22 Papers of the NAACP, Part 27.

23 Students for a Democratic Society, "Chester, PA: Community Organization in the Other America," MS, Delaware County Historical Society, Chester, Pa., December 4, 1963.

24 Bender, *Police Brutality in Chester*, 4–5.

25 Governor's Commission Investigating Recent Events in Chester, Pennsylvania, *Report of the Commission*.

26 *Delaware County Daily Times*, "Negroes Form New Group Called ACT," March 16, 1964.

27 *Delaware County Daily Times*, "NAACP Blasts Malcolm X," March 14, 1964.

28 Ibid.

29 Papers of the NAACP, Part 27.

30 Papers of the NAACP, Part 25, *Branch Department Files*, Series B, *Regional Files and Special Reports, 1956–1965*.

31 Pope et al., "Chester, PA," 3.

32 Governor's Commission Investigating Recent Events in Chester, Pennsylvania, *Report of the Commission*, 29.

33 Bender, *Police Brutality in Chester*, 4.

34 Ibid.

35 Ibid., 10–11.

36 Governor's Commission Investigating Recent Events in Chester, Pennsylvania, *Report of the Commission*, 36.

37 Bender, *Police Brutality in Chester*, 24.

38 Governor's Commission Investigating Recent Events in Chester, Pennsylvania, *Report of the Commission*, 62.

39 John R. Fry, "Remember Chester," *Presbyterian Life*, June 1964, 6.

40 Ibid.

41 Papers of the NAACP, Part 25.

42 Governor's Commission Investigating Recent Events in Chester, Pennsylvania, *Report of the Commission*.

43 Ibid., 93.

44 Ibid., 14–15.

45 *Pennsylvania Human Relations Commission v. Chester School District* (1967).

46 *Delaware County Daily Times*, "CFFN Frowns on CPA 'Self-Help,'" July 30, 1964.

47 Kirk Byron Jones, "The Activism of Interpretation: Black Pastors and Public Life," *Christian Century*, September 13–20, 1989, 817–818.

48 Governor's Commission Investigating Recent Events in Chester, Pennsylvania, *Report of the Commission*, 91.

49 Papers of the NAACP, Part 27.

50 Bender, *Police Brutality in Chester*, 6.

51 Governor's Commission Investigating Recent Events in Chester, Pennsylvania, *Report of the Commission*, 12.

52 Spencer Klaw, "Old Scratchhead Wakes Up in Chester, Pennsylvania," *Reporter Magazine*, June 18, 1964, 34.

53 Bender, *Police Brutality in Chester*, 6; Governor's Commission Investigating Recent Events in Chester, Pennsylvania, *Report of the Commission*, 12.

54 Papers of the NAACP, Part 23.

55 Ibid.

56 Klaw, "Old Scratchhead," 33.

57 McLarnon, "Ruling Suburbia," 561.

58 Ibid.

59 Ibid., 560.

60 Ibid., 563.

61 *Delaware County Daily Times*, "Civil Rights Vacuum in Our City," January 4, 1967.

62 George W. Corner, "The Black Coalition: An Experiment in Racial Cooperation, Philadelphia, 1968," *Proceedings of the American Philosophical Society* 120, no. 3 (1976): 178–186.

63 Greater Chester Movement, "Greater Chester Movement Policy Statement," November 11, 1961, 3.

64 Ibid., 6.

65 Ibid.

66 Ibid.

67 John Thomas Meli, "Barriers to Employment Growth in a Distressed Area: A Case Study of Chester, Pennsylvania," Delaware County Archives, Lima, Pa., December 11, 1972, MS.

68 *Delaware County Daily Times*, "Scott to Hire, Train 30 Poor," July 26, 1968.

69 Robert Zdnek, "Community Development Corporations," in Severyn T. Bruyn and James Meehan, eds., *Beyond the Market and the State: New Directions in Community Development* (Philadelphia: Temple University Press, 1987), 112–127.

70 Ira Katznelson, *City Trenches: Urban Politics and the Patterning of Class in the United States* (New York: Pantheon, 1981); Keith Lawrence, "Expanding Comprehensiveness: Structural Racism and Community Building in the United States," in John Pierson and Joan Smith, eds., *Rebuilding Community: Policy and Practice in Urban Regeneration* (New York: Palgrave, 2001), 34–63; Alice O'Connor, "Swimming against the Tide: A Brief History of Federal Policy in Poor Communities," in Ronald Ferguson and William T. Dickens, eds., *Urban Problems and Community Development* (Washington, D.C.: Brookings Institution Press, 1999), 77–110.

CHAPTER 5. FIVE SQUARE MILES OF HELL

1 Douglas L. Massey and Nancy A. Denton, *American Apartheid: Segregation and the Making of the Underclass* (Cambridge, Mass.: Harvard University Press, 1993).

2 *Delaware County Daily Times*, "Probe GCM Immediately," February 26, 1969.

3 *Delaware County Daily Times*, "After $12.4 Million, City's Poor Still Poor," May 1, 1972.

4 *Delaware County Daily Times*, "Relatives Find GCM a Good Place to Work," May 5, 1972.

5 *Delaware County Daily Times*, "Board Members' Businesses Thrive with Sales to GCM," May 3, 1972.

6 McLarnon, "Ruling Suburbia," 601.

7 *Delaware County Daily Times*, "GCM Buys Insurance from Board Member," May 2, 1972.

8 *Delaware County Daily Times*, "No Laughing Matter to Poor," May 9, 1972.

9 *Delaware County Daily Times*, "Action Centers Reach Few," May 10, 1972.

10 *Delaware County Daily Times*, "City Hall Pulls GCM Strings," May 8, 1972.

11 Pennsylvania Human Relations Commission, *Annual Report* (Harrisburg: Pennsylvania Human Relations Commission, 1968), 9.

12 Ibid., 12.

13 Ibid.

14 Ibid., 54–58.

15 Pennsylvania Crime Commission, *Pennsylvania Crime Commission 1971 Report*, Commonwealth of Pennsylvania, Department of Justice, December 1971.

16 Ibid.

17 *Delaware County Daily Times*, "GCM Loses Out on CITGO Venture," May 16, 1972.

18 Ibid.

19 Pennsylvania Crime Commission, "A Chester City Racketeer: Hidden Interests Revealed," Commonwealth of Pennsylvania, Department of Justice, March 1978.

20 Ibid.

21 Gregory T. Magarity, "RICO Investigations: A Case Study," *American Criminal Law Review* 17 (1979): 367–378.

22 *Delaware County Daily Times*, "Sprague Report Says No County Corruption," October 18, 1974.

23 *Delaware County Daily Times*, "State Asks Prosecutor to 'Review' Delco," July 23, 1975.

24 *United States of America v. John H. Nacrelli* (1979).

25 Pennsylvania Crime Commission, *Organized Crime in Pennsylvania: A Decade of Change* (Conshohocken: Pennsylvania Crime Commission, 1990), 315.

26 Magarity, "RICO Investigations," 373.

27 Pennsylvania Crime Commission, *Organized Crime in Pennsylvania*, 310.

28 Ibid., 211.

29 Charles H. Rogovin and Frederick T. Martens, "The Role of Crime Commissions in Organized Crime Control," in Robert J. Kelley, Ko-Lin Chin, and Rufus Schatzberg, eds., *Handbook of Organized Crime in the United States* (Westport, Conn.: Greenwood, 1994), 389–400.

30 Sheila Foster, "Justice from the Ground Up: Distributive Inequities, Grassroots Resistance, and the Transformative Politics of the Environmental Justice Movement," *California Law Review* 86, no. 4 (1998): 775.

31 *Philadelphia Inquirer*, "A Trash Plan They're Willing to Fight to Get," September 28, 1986; *Philadelphia Inquirer*, "Delco OKs Trash Plant in Chester," November 26, 1986.

32 *Delaware County Daily Times*, "Chester Trash Project," June 12, 1989; *Philadelphia Inquirer*, "Vote Delayed on Chester Trash Plant," November 4, 1986; Jerome Balter, "Environmental Justice: Time for Meaningful Action," *Temple Environmental Law and Technology Journal* 18 (1999): 153.

33 *Philadelphia Inquirer*, "Suspect Bond Issues Put Communities in a Bind," June 29, 1987.

34 *Philadelphia Inquirer*, "A Trash Plan."

35 *Philadelphia Inquirer*, "Chester's Mayor Asks Residents to Vacate Homes for Trash Plant," July 1, 1987.

36 *Philadelphia Inquirer*, "Dealing with Trash: A Tale of Two Plants," August 30, 1987.

37 *Philadelphia Inquirer*, "Delco Sheriff Rebuffed on Trash-Plant Proposal," December 11, 1986.

38 *Philadelphia Inquirer*, "$335,000 Fee for Chester Counsel Raises Questions," December 24, 1986; *Philadelphia Inquirer*, "Questions on Funding Trash Plant: Unusual Method Cited in Chester Bond Sale," February 1, 1987.

39 *Philadelphia Inquirer*, "Questions on Funding Trash Plant"; *Philadelphia Inquirer*, "Suspect Bond Issues."

40 *Philadelphia Inquirer*, "Dealing with Trash."

41 *Philadelphia Inquirer*, "IRS Tells Another City to Pay over Bond Deal," March 15, 1991; *Philadelphia Inquirer*, "Grand Jury Accusations Deal Chester Another Blow," April 14, 1991.

42 *Philadelphia Inquirer*, "Mayor Says Chester Won't Pay IRS," February 28, 1991.

43 *Philadelphia Inquirer*, "A Trash Plan."

44 *Philadelphia Inquirer*, "Vote Delayed on Chester Trash Plant"; *Philadelphia Inquirer*, "PE in Deal for Power from Trash, Westinghouse Plans Chester Waste Plant," June 10, 1988; Foster, "Justice from the Ground Up"; Luke W. Cole and Sheila R. Foster, *From the Ground Up: Environmental Racism and the Rise of the Environmental Justice Movement* (New York: NYU Press, 2001).

45 *Philadelphia Inquirer*, "Delco Sheriff Rebuffed."

46 *Philadelphia Inquirer*, "Tangle of Trash Plans for Chester," April 24, 1988.

47 *Philadelphia Inquirer*, "No Matter What, It's Still Home," July 9, 1987.

48 *Philadelphia Inquirer*, "Chester's Mayor Asks Residents to Vacate Homes."

49 Ibid.

50 Edward J. Walsh, Rex Warland, and D. Clayton Smith, *Don't Burn It Here: Grassroots Challenges to Waste Incinerators* (University Park: Pennsylvania State University Press, 1997).

51 *Philadelphia Inquirer*, "Minister Critical of Delco Plan," May 18, 1988.

52 *Philadelphia Inquirer*, "An Ocean of Opposition to Trash Plant," May 1, 1988.

53 *Philadelphia Inquirer*, "Councilman Files Libel Suit in Trash Plant Battle," July 7, 1988.

54 Ibid.

55 *Philadelphia Inquirer*, "Delco's Proposal for Trash Plant Expected to Gain Approval of State," August 25, 1988; *Philadelphia Inquirer*, "In Raucous Meeting, Chester Mayor and Council Battle over Trash Plant," August 13, 1988.

56 *Philadelphia Inquirer*, "Chester OKs a County Trash Plant," November 17, 1988; *Philadelphia Inquirer*, "Chester Begins to Collect on Trash-to-Steam Plant," February 2, 1989.

57 *Philadelphia Inquirer*, "Chester Official Gets Prison Term in Trash-to-Steam Kickback Case," September 6, 1992.

58 *Delaware County Daily Times*, "What Do You Think about Chester?" February 19, 1998.

59 Cole and Foster, *From the Ground Up*, 30–34.

60 Pennsylvania Crime Commission, *Pennsylvania Crime Commission 1989 Report*, Commonwealth of Pennsylvania, Department of Justice, 1989.

61 *Philadelphia Inquirer*, "In Feudal Chester, Ex-Mayor Retains a Shadowy Rule," February 6, 1989; *Philadelphia Inquirer*, "Report: Nacrelli Involved in Trash Plant Talks," March 2, 1989; *Philadelphia Inquirer*, "Catania Says He Met with Nacrelli," March 9, 1989.

62 Cole and Foster, *From the Ground Up*, 38.

63 U.S. Census Bureau, *Census of Population and Housing, 1950* (Washington, D.C.: U.S. Census Bureau, 1950); U.S. Census Bureau, *Census of Population and Housing, 1990* (Washington, D.C.: U.S. Census Bureau, 1990); Mike Ewall, Campus Coalition concerning Chester (C-4), "Environmental Racism in Chester," 1999, www.ejnet.org.

64 Barry E. Hill, "Chester, Pennsylvania: Was It a Classic Example of Environmental Injustice?" *Vermont Law Review* 23 (1998): 479–510; Foster, "Justice from the Ground Up," 775–841; Jerome Balter, "The EPA Needs a Workable Environmental Justice Protocol," *Tulane Environmental Law Journal* 12 (1998): 357–375; Balter, "Environmental Justice," 153–179.

65 Michael Greenberg and Dona Schneider, *Environmentally Devastated Neighborhoods: Perceptions, Policies, and Realities* (New Brunswick, N.J.: Rutgers University Press, 1996), 90–94.

66 Meta Mendel-Reyes, *Reclaiming Democracy: The Sixties in Politics and Memory* (New York: Routledge, 1995), 155.

67 Judith Auer Shaw, "Siting Incinerators in Neighborhoods: How Much Environmental Justice Do Residents Get?" Ph.D. diss., Rutgers University (2002); Cole and Foster, *From the Ground Up*.

68 U.S. Environmental Protection Agency and Pennsylvania Department of Environmental Resources, "Environmental Risk Study for City of Chester, PA,"

1995; Chester Environmental Justice Factsheet, 1996, www.ejnet.org. In Chester the question of racial discrimination as intentional or manifest in the uneven consequences of siting came to the fore in a landmark legal battle over the clustering of waste facilities in the city's West End. See court briefs from *Chester Residents v. Department of Environmental Protection* (1995); *Chester Residents for Quality Living v. Seif* (1996); *Chester Residents for Quality Living v. Seif* (1997). See also Hill, "Chester, Pennsylvania"; Foster, "Justice from the Ground Up"; Robert W. Collin and Robin Morris Collin, "The Role of Communities in Environmental Decisions: Communities Speaking for Themselves," *Journal of Environmental Law and Litigation* 13 (1998): 38; Balter, "The EPA Needs a Workable Environmental Justice Protocol"; Kristen L. Raney, "The Role of Title VI in *Chester Residents v. Seif*: Is the Future of Environmental Justice Really Brighter?" *Journal of Natural Resources and Environmental Law* 14 (1998): 135–151; Bradford C. Mank, "Is There a Private Cause of Action under EPA's Title VI Regulations? The Need to Empower Environmental Justice Plaintiffs," *Columbia Journal of Environmental Law* 1 (1999): 1–61; Valerie P. Mahoney, "Environmental Justice: From Partial Victories to Complete Solutions," *Cardozo Law Review* 21 (1999): 361–411; Amanda C. L. Vig, "Using Title VI to Salvage Civil Rights from Waste: *Chester Residents Concerned for Quality Living v. Seif*, 132 F.3d 925 (3d Cir. 1997)," *University of Cincinnati Law Review* 67 (1999): 907–934; Uma Outka, "Environmental Injustice and the Problem of the Law," *Maine Law Review* 57 (2005): 209–259.

69 Balter, "The EPA Needs a Workable Environmental Justice Protocol"; Balter, "Environmental Justice"; Vig, "Using Title VI"; Mahoney, "Environmental Justice"; Robert Bahar and George McCollough, *Laid to Waste: A Chester Neighborhood Fights for Its Future* (Berkeley, Calif.: Media, 1997).

70 Balter, "Environmental Justice"; Collin and Collin, "The Role of Communities in Environmental Decisions."

71 *Chester Residents Concerned for Quality Living v. Seif* (1996); *Chester Residents Concerned for Quality Living v. Seif* (1997); Mank, "Is There a Private Cause of Action?"

72 Daniel Isales, "Environmental Justice and Title VI: The Administrative Remedy," *Temple Environmental Law and Technology Journal* 18 (1999): 125–176; Melissa Kiniyalocts, *Environmental Justice: Avoiding the Difficulty of Proving Discriminatory Intent in Hazardous Waste Siting Decisions* (Madison: University of Wisconsin-Madison, Land Tenure Center, 2000); Shaw, "Siting Incinerators in Neighborhoods."

73 Isales, "Environmental Justice and Title VI"; Mahoney, "Environmental Justice." The Supreme Court's dismissal left open the right of private parties to sue the state to enforce regulations under Title VI when there was unintentional discrimination. In April 2001, however, the Supreme Court ruled in *Alexander et al. v. Sandoval* that private citizens cannot use Title VI of the 1964 Civil

Rights Act to sue state agencies for unintentional discrimination. For environmental social movements deploying a legal strategy, the burden of proving intentional racism remains. See John DiBari, "How the *Sandoval* Ruling Will Affect Environmental Justice Plaintiffs," *St. John's Law Review* 76 (2002): 1019–1046; Olga D. Pomar and Luke W. Cole, "Camden, New Jersey, and the Struggle for Environmental Justice," *Clearinghouse Review* 36 (2002): 94–108.

CHAPTER 6. WELCOME TO THE "POST-RACIAL" BLACK CITY

1 Craig Offman, "The 10 Most Corrupt Cities in America," *George Magazine*, March 1998.

2 The ordinance did not prevent existing waste facilities from increasing their intakes of trash. In the fall of 2015 the city's Covanta waste incinerator contracted to burn trash from New York City.

3 The phrase is a reverse of the title of Elvin K. Wyly and Daniel J. Hammel, "Islands of Decay in Seas of Renewal: Housing Policy and the Resurgence of Gentrification," *Housing Policy Debate* 10, no. 4 (1999): 711–771.

4 David Wilson, "Social Justice and Neoliberal Discourse," *Southeastern Geographer* 47, no. 1 (2007): 7–100; Gerard Dumenil and Dominique Levy, "The Nature and Contradictions of Neoliberalism," in Leo Panitch, Colin Leys, Alan Zuege, and Martijn Konings, eds., *The Globalization Decade: A Critical Reader* (London: Merlin, 2004), 245–274.

5 FAIR Deal Coalition of Chester, "Rolling the Dice: Gambling with Chester's Future," September 2006, www.fairdealchester.org.

6 Pennsylvania Department of Transportation, www.penndot.gov.

7 *Delaware County Daily Times*, "Storm Clouds Loom on the Waterfront," January 2, 2009.

8 *Delaware County Daily Times*, "Gambling on Chester: City on the Move?" December 22, 2007.

9 CEDA official, interview with the author, 2009; residents associated with Action United, a nonprofit organization that helped residents organize on the supermarket and other community issues, interviews with the author.

10 Neubeck and Cazenave, *Welfare Racism*.

11 David O. Sears, P. J. Henry, and Rick Kosterman, "Egalitarian Values and Contemporary Racial Politics," in David O. Sears, James Sidanius, and Lawrence Bobo, eds., *Racialized Politics: The Debate about Racism in America* (Chicago: University of Chicago Press, 2000), 103.

12 Henry A. Giroux, "Spectacles of Race and Pedagogies of Denial: Anti-Black Racist Pedagogy under the Reign of Neoliberalism," *Communication Education* 52, nos. 3–4 (2003): 191–211.

13 Ibid., 198.

14 Ibid., 195–196.

15 Christopher Mele, "Revisiting the Citadel and the Ghetto: Legibility, Race, and Contemporary Urban Development," *Sociology of Race and Ethnicity* (2016); doi:10.1177/2332649215608874

16 Marty Moss-Coane, "Chester: Murders, Curfews, and Violence Prevention," *Radio Times*, July 13, 2010, http://whyy.org; Erik Eckholm, "A City Celebrates a Brand New Stadium, but Not after 9 P.M. in Some Quarters," *New York Times*, June 27, 2010.

17 Zygmunt Bauman, *Consuming Life* (Cambridge, U.K.: Polity, 2007), 126–127.

18 See Jessica Shannon Cobb and Kimberly Kay Hoang, "Protagonist-Driven Urban Ethnography," *City and Community* 14, no. 4 (2015): 348–351; Mario L. Small, "De-Exoticizing Ghetto Poverty: On the Ethics of Representation in Urban Ethnography," *City and Community* 14, no. 4 (2015): 352–358.

INDEX

ABOUT THE AUTHOR

Christopher Mele is an urban sociologist at the University at Buffalo. He is the author of *Selling the Lower East Side: Culture, Real Estate, and Resistance in New York City* (2000), co-editor (with Robert Adelman) of *Race, Space, and Exclusion: Segregation and Beyond in Metropolitan America* (2015), and co-editor (with Jan Lin) of *The Urban Sociology Reader*, 2nd edition (2012).